wa ways handbook

Revised and updated 2003

Course devised by Andrew Newman, Willow Wren Training.

Illustrations and design by Pete Galvin.
Photos courtesy of Blakes Holiday Boating, Broom, Gary Blake and Paul Bullock.

We recommend that you carry the relevant navigation handbook on board for the areas you intend to cruise.

The RYA is committed to encouraging both women and men to participate in boating. For clarity only, the text in this handbook is written using the masculine gender eg. Man Overboard.

This book is not all inclusive of every term or name for items as there are regional variations.

Published by
The Royal Yachting Association
RYA House, Ensign Way
Hamble, Southampton SO31 4YA
Tel: 0845 345 0400 Fax: 0845 345 0329
Email: info@rya.org.uk Web: www.rya.org.uk

ACKNOWLEDGEMENTS

The RYA would like to thank the following organisations for their assistance with this new edition and their support in endorsing it to their members and the public.

Association of Waterways Cruising Clubs (AWCC)

Email:info@awcc.org.uk
Website: www.awcc.org.uk

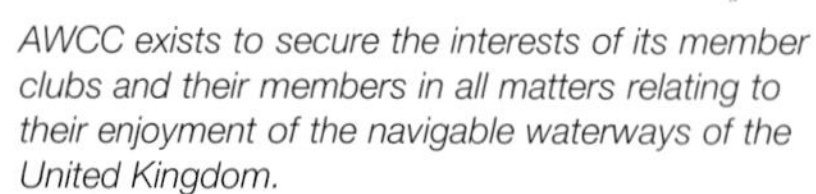

AWCC exists to secure the interests of its member clubs and their members in all matters relating to their enjoyment of the navigable waterways of the United Kingdom.

The Barge Association (DBA)

Port Werburgh, Vicarage Lane, Hoo,
Rochester, Kent, ME3 9TW
Tel: 07000 227437
Email: info@barges.org
Website: www.barges.org

The DBA aims to bring together people interested in barges and barging, both in the UK and Europe.

British Marine Federation (BMF)

Marine House, Thorpe Lea Road,
Egham, Surrey TW20 8BF
Tel: 01784 223600
Email: info@britishmarine.co.uk
Wesite: www.britishmarine.co.uk

The British Marine Federation is the trade association for businesses operating in the UK marine industry. With more than1500 member companies, it represents over 75 per cent of the industry's turnover. The British Marine Federation is recognized by the government as the voice of the UK boating industry.

British Waterways

Willow Grange, Church Road,
Watford WD17 4QA
Tel: 01923 201120 f 201400
Email: enquiries.hq@britishwaterways.co.uk
Website: www.britishwaterwaysco.uk

British Waterways cares for 2,000 miles of canals and rivers nationwide. The publicly owned corporation works with a broad range of private and public sector partners to bring the economic, social and environmental benefits of restored and regenerated waterways to millions of people across the country and to develop the waterways as a leading leisure and recreational destination.

Broads Authority

18 Colegate, Norwich
Norfolk NR3 1BQ
Tel: 01603 610734 Fax: 01603 765710
Email: broads@broads-authority.gov.uk
Website: broads-authority.gov.uk

The Broads Authority has the status of a national park authority and manages the 125 miles of inland rivers and 40 broads (shallow lakes) for conservation, navigation and recreation.

Canal Boat & Inland Waterways Magazine

4 The Courtyard, Denmark Street,
Wokingham, Berkshire RG40 2AZ
Tel: 0118 977 1677
Email: canalboat@goring.co.uk
www.canalboatmagazine.com

Canal Boat & Inland Waterways is a monthly magazine for newcomers to the rivers and canals, and existing boaters alike.

The Environment Agency

Rio House, Waterside Drive,
Aztec West, Almondsbury,
Bristol BS32 4UD
Tel: 01454 624411 Fax: 01454 624014
Email: enquiries@environment-agency.gov.uk
Website: www.environment-agency.gov.uk

The Environment Agency's aim is to manage the healthy growth of waterways for leisure, business, local communities and wildlife.

Inland Waterways Association

3 Norfolk Court, Norfolk Road,
Rickmansworth, WD3 1LT
Tel: 01923 711114 Fax: 01923 897000
E-mail: iwa@waterways.org.uk
Website: www.waterways.org.uk

For nearly 60 years, The Inland Waterways Association and its thousands of members have campaigned for the conservation, use, maintenance, restoration and sensitive development of Britain's canals and river navigations.

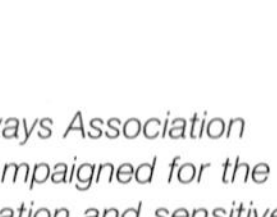

National Association of Boat Owners (NABO)

Freepost (BM8367),
Birmingham, B31 2BR
Email: gen.sec@nabo.org.uk
Website: www.nabo.org.uk

NABO is an association body that represents boat owners on inland and estuarial waters.

Britain's Inland Waterways were built in the 18th and 19th centuries as a new transport system, and enjoyed great prosperity for many years. However, with the advent of the railways, use of the waterways slowly declined and by the end of the Second World War many canals were derelict. Rivers fared somewhat better thanks to the new Victorian passion for pleasure cruising in the late 1800s.

In 1946, the Inland Waterways Association was founded and enthusiasts countrywide started campaigning to rescue our canal heritage.

Now, more than 50 years later, there are over 3,000 miles of canals and navigable rivers for us to use and enjoy for leisure and relaxation.

Each year, more and more people discover the delights of inland boating and we hope that this handbook, and the RYA training course which accompanies it, will help to make your waterway experience more fun, enjoyable and safe.

Whenever you go boating, take this handbook with you for quick and easy reference, along with the navigation booklet for the waterways you intend to visit.

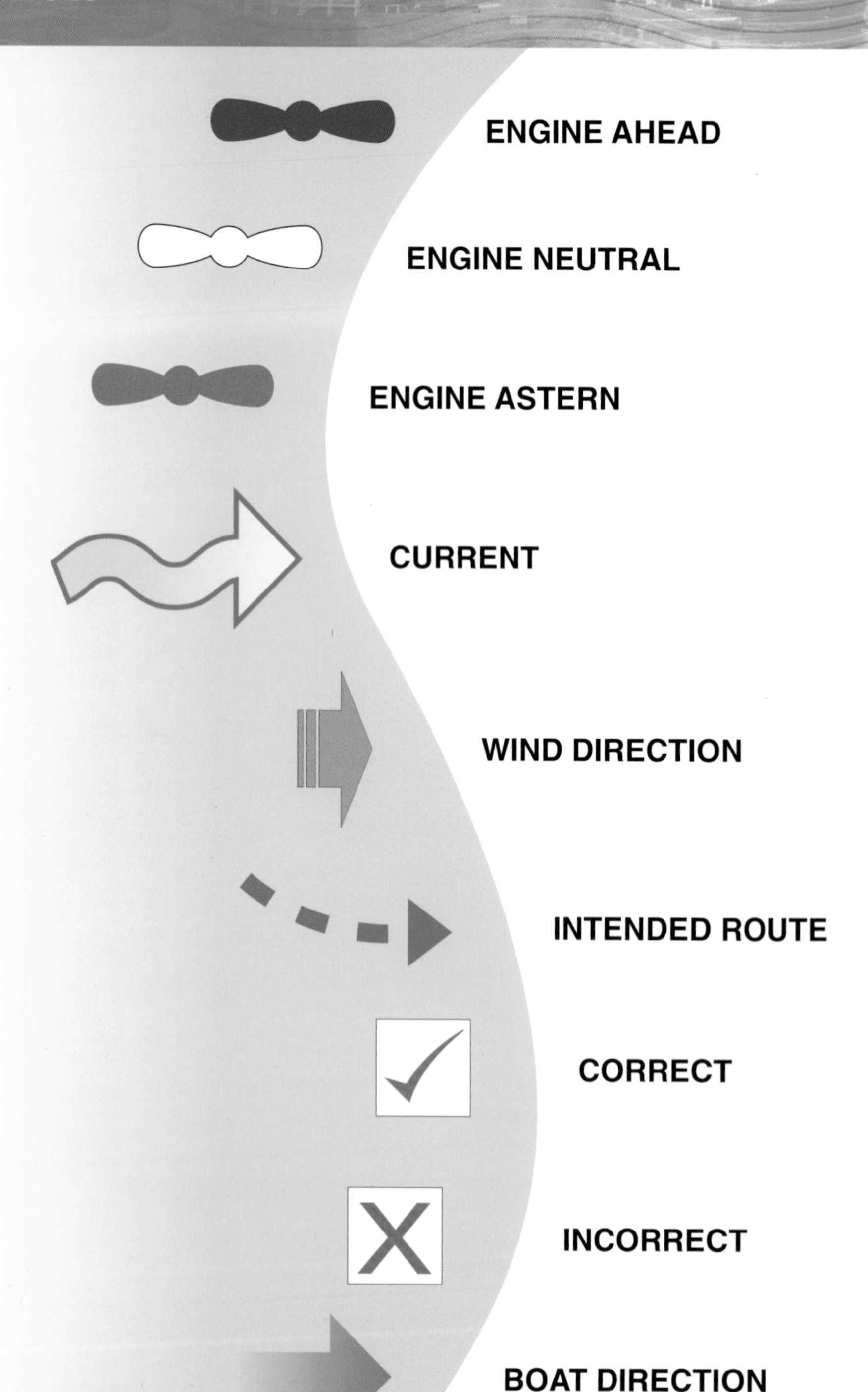
ENGINE AHEAD
ENGINE NEUTRAL
ENGINE ASTERN
CURRENT
WIND DIRECTION
INTENDED ROUTE
CORRECT
INCORRECT
BOAT DIRECTION

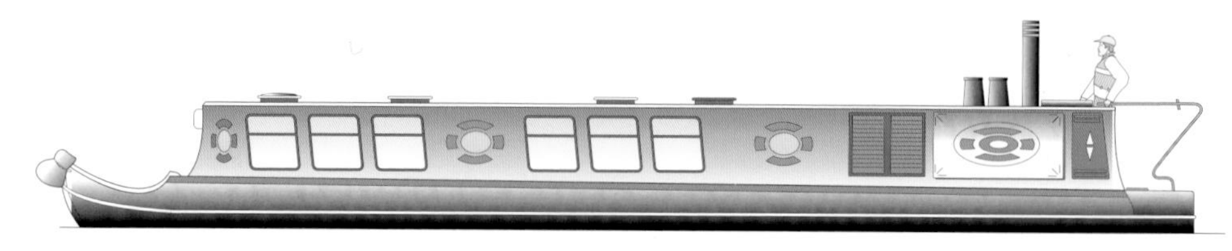

TRADITIONAL NARROWBOAT

Suitable for most narrow and broad canals and rivers.
Up to 70 feet long. (maximum length for most canals).

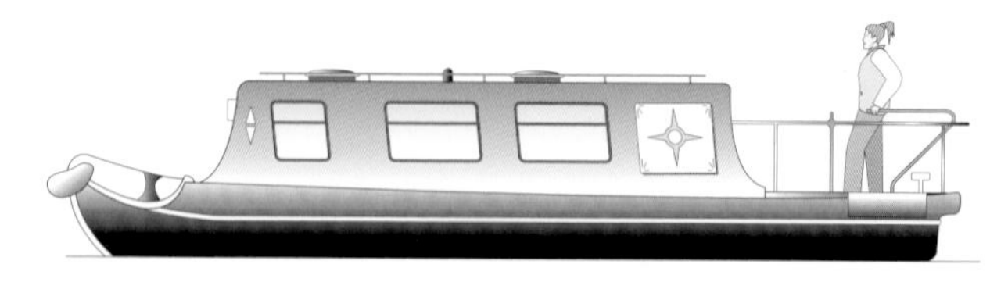

CANAL CRUISER

Usually has a larger rear deck, ideal for the family.
Both types have steel hulls and are suitable for use on narrow canals.

BROAD BEAM and DUTCH BARGES

Large craft, comfortable as a live-aboard vessel often used abroad.

WIDE BEAM INLAND CRUISER

(CENTRE COCKPIT)

Both of the above and below types are popular on the Norfolk Broads,
Thames and other larger waterways.
The wind can effect steering control on both designs.

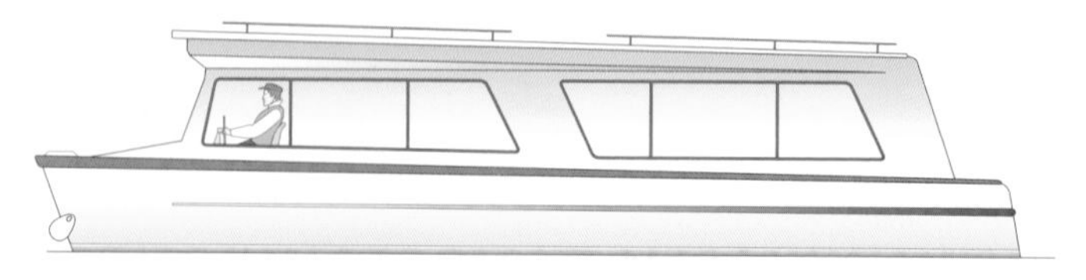

FORWARD STEERING CRUISER

On forward-steering cruisers, the stern is harder to control
and see when manoeuvring.

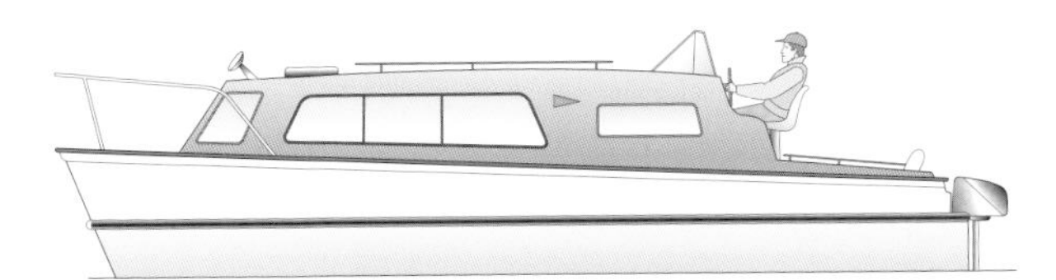

SMALL NARROW BEAM OUTBOARD CRUISER

Very popular on canals and smaller rivers. Economical to buy and run. Easy to steer and trailable. The vunerable outboard motor can be a disadvantage.

ELECTRIC LAUNCH

Electric power is growing in popularity for inland craft, as it is silent, and causes no pollution to the local environment, or annoyance to other users of the waterway.

SEA / ESTUARY OUTBOARD CRUISER

Good beginner's boat. Inexpensive to buy and trailable. Ideal for weekends away spent exploring isolated waterways.

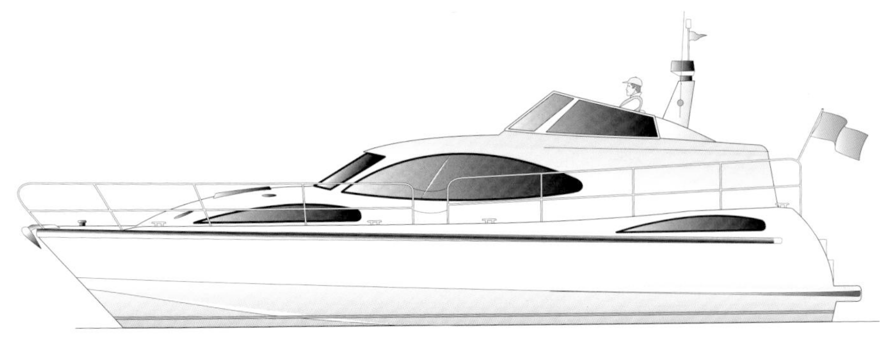

SEA / ESTUARY CRUISER

Popular on wide rivers. Well equipped, comfortable and powerful, but expensive to buy and run. Capable of sea passages. Limited inland use due to height and width restrictions.

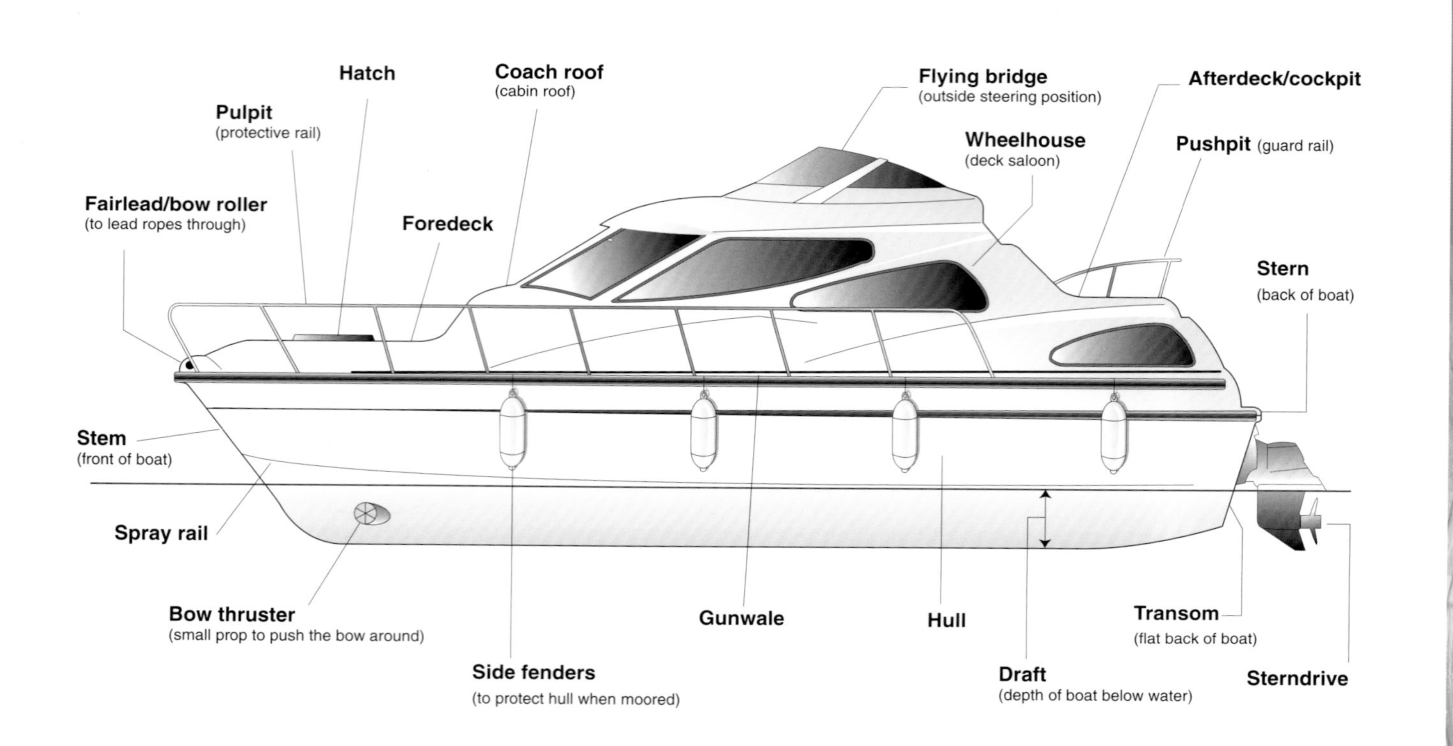
Hatch
Coach roof
(cabin roof)
Flying bridge
(outside steering position)
Afterdeck/cockpit
Pulpit
(protective rail)
Wheelhouse
(deck saloon)
Pushpit (guard rail)
Fairlead/bow roller
(to lead ropes through)
Foredeck
Stern
(back of boat)
Stem
(front of boat)
Spray rail
Bow thruster
(small prop to push the bow around)
Gunwale
Hull
Transom
(flat back of boat)
Side fenders
(to protect hull when moored)
Draft
(depth of boat below water)
Sterndrive

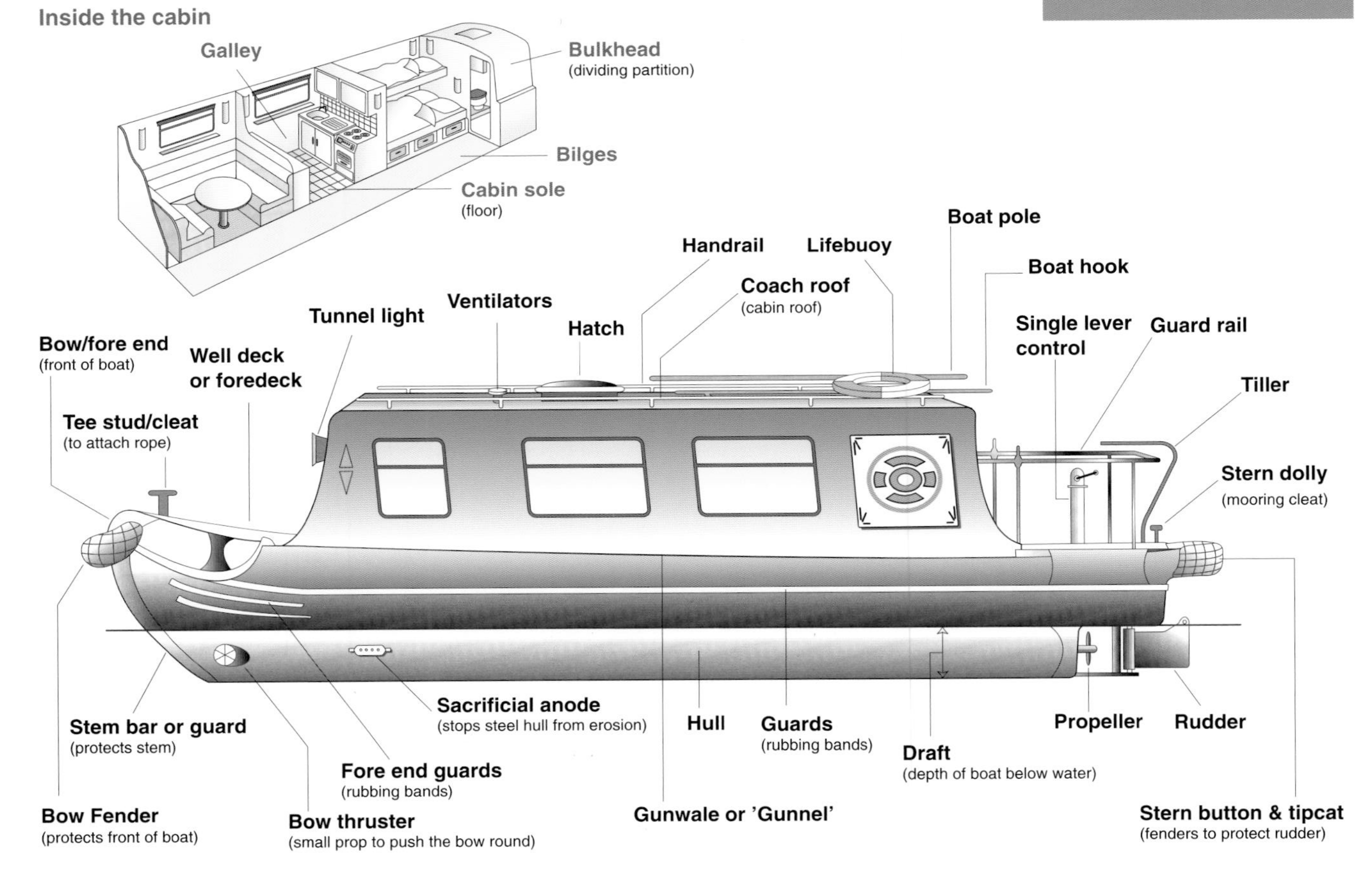

Inside the cabin
Galley
Bulkhead
(dividing partition)
Bilges
Cabin sole
(floor)
Boat pole
Handrail
Lifebuoy
Boat hook
Coach roof
(cabin roof)
Tunnel light
Ventilators
Hatch
Bow/fore end
(front of boat)
Well deck
or foredeck
Single lever
control
Guard rail
Tiller
Tee stud/cleat
(to attach rope)
Stern dolly
(mooring cleat)
Sacrificial anode
(stops steel hull from erosion)
Stem bar or guard
(protects stem)
Hull
Guards
(rubbing bands)
Propeller
Rudder
Draft
(depth of boat below water)
Fore end guards
(rubbing bands)
Bow Fender
(protects front of boat)
Bow thruster
(small prop to push the bow round)
Gunwale or 'Gunnel'
Stern button & tipcat
(fenders to protect rudder)

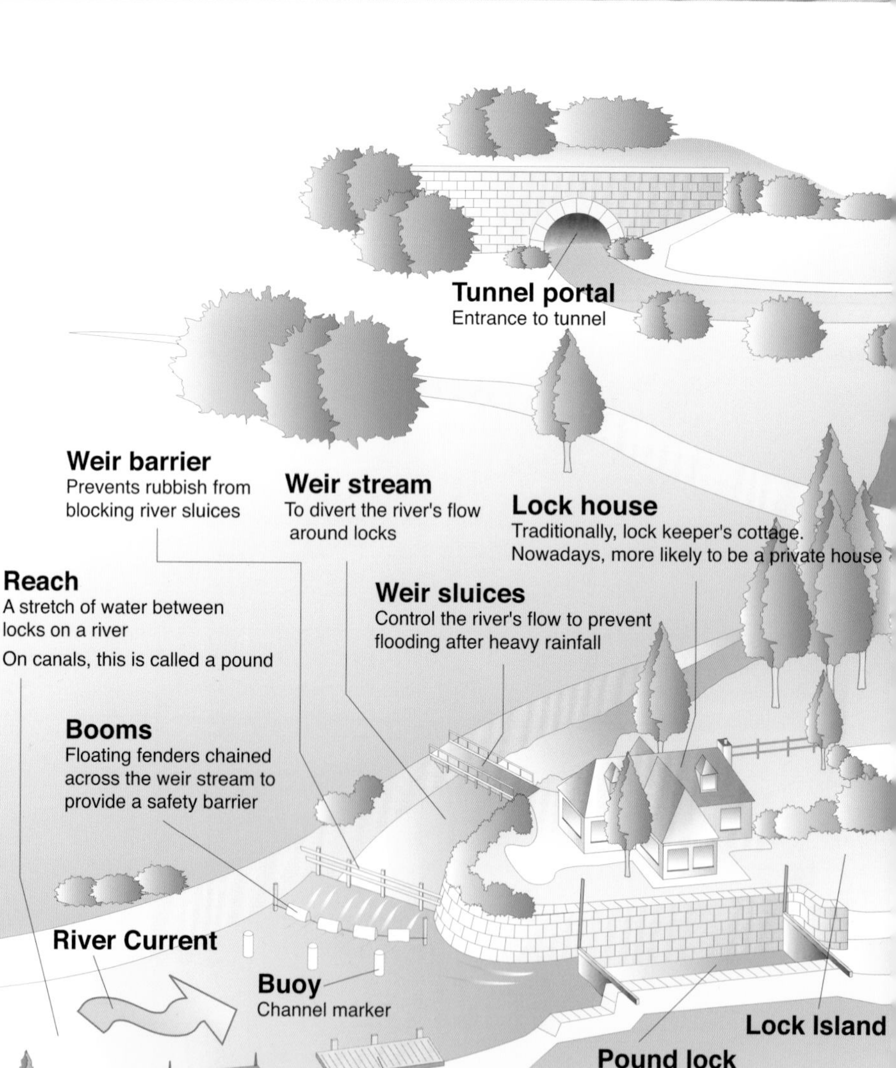

RIVER

Rivers flow where nature intends, following their natural course, through valleys of their own making, down towards the sea. When a river current is too strong for navigation, locks will gently 'ease' boats up or down hill.

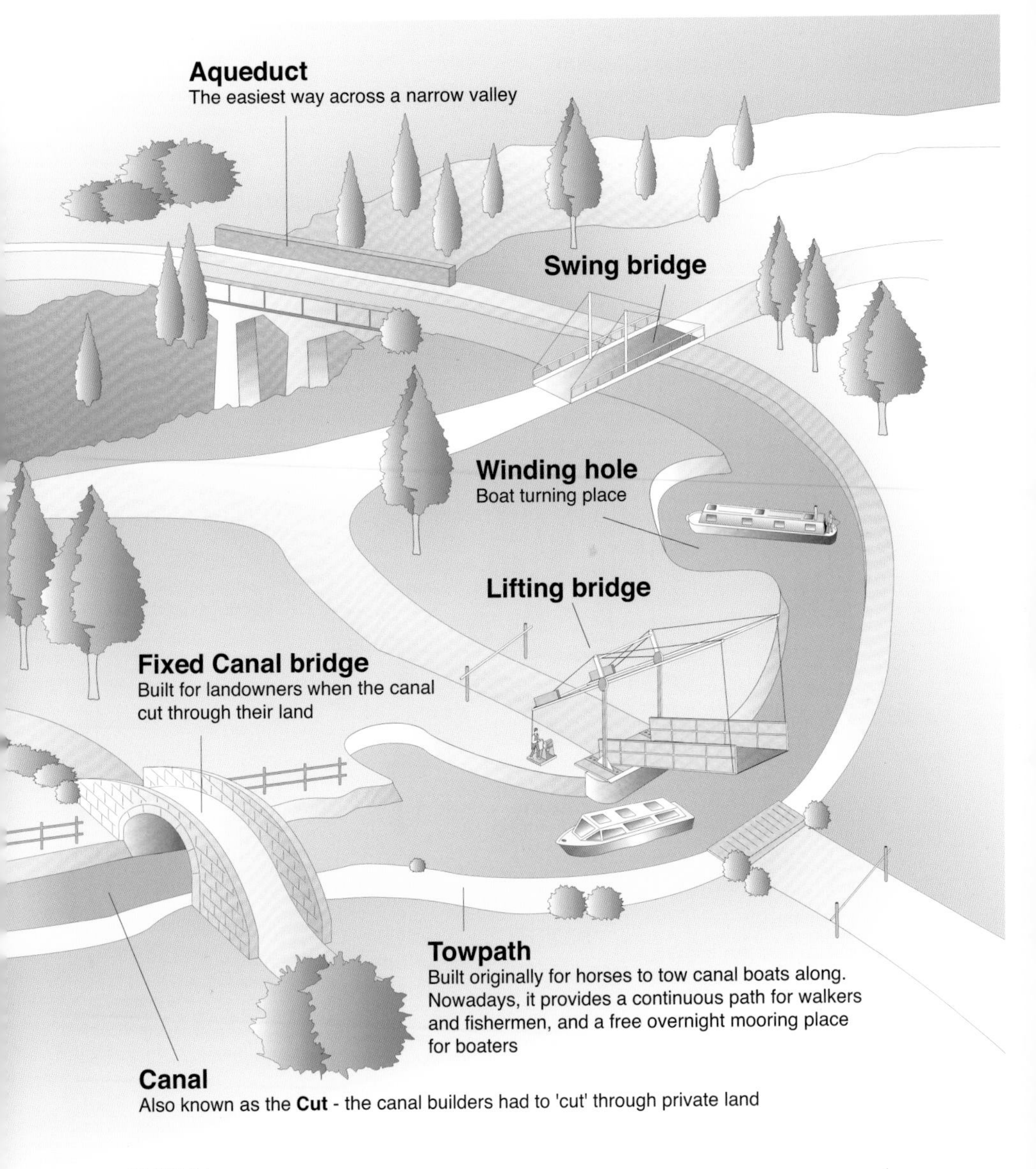

CANAL

Canals were built to take boats where no river could go - across valleys, and over or through hills. Locks 'lift' boats up or down hill.

Before you set off

- Check that your boat is in good condition. All boats should meet the Boat Safety Scheme standards. These are boat construction standards and regular tests required by licence holders on nearly all inland waterways.
- Ensure that you and your crew know how to handle the boat and the conditions you may encounter on your cruise.
- Get local information from the navigation authority before going onto unfamiliar waterways. On rivers, check information on tidal or current conditions.
- Plan your cruise. Allow plenty of time so you can always arrive in daylight. It's not advisable to cruise after dark or in bad visibility. When working out your schedule, take into account the speed restrictions.
- Check that your water and fuel tanks are full.

Equipment checklist

Make sure that you and the crew know where to find the following:

- Lifebelt. Lifeline *(if supplied)*.
- Lifejackets.
- Anchor. *For rivers, the rope and chain should be a combined length of at least six times the deepest part of the river.*
- Fire extinguishers and fire blanket.
- Emergency shut-offs for battery, gas and fuel.
- Bilge pump.
- Emergency torch.
- Mooring ropes – *long enough to stretch from your boat to the bollard and back in a deep lock.*
- Mooring stakes and hammer.
- Horn.
- First aid kit.
- Boat pole and/or hook.
- Two windlasses *(handles for operating locks.)*

Lifejackets

There is quite a difference between the various types of buoyancy aids and lifejackets. In general terms:

- A buoyancy aid is designed to keep a conscious person afloat.
- An automatically inflating lifejacket is designed to support an unconscious person afloat, with their nose and mouth clear of the water.

Children's lifejackets (100N) should be fitted with crutch straps, so the jacket stays on if the child has to be lifted out of the water, and D-rings to allow harness lines to be attached.

It is sensible to wear a life jacket, especially near locks, deep or fast flowing water and at night. We recommend that children, non-swimmers and those with disabilities wear a lifejacket at all times.

Children

Ensure that children are supervised at all times on or off the boat. This is especially important around locks.

What to wear

- Loose, casual clothing.
- Non-slip shoes are most suitable for wet slippery lock areas and muddy towpaths. (Some deck shoes have poor grip on wet grass).
- Waterproof clothing is also advisable as most canal boats have outside steering positions, and tunnels drip.
- As with any outdoor pursuits, sunhats, sunglasses, and suitable sun block are highly recommended.

INLAND CRUISING IS AN EXTREMELY SAFE PASTIME BUT THE FOLLOWING PRECAUTIONS SHOULD BE TAKEN:

Be aware

- Make sure that your crew know the importance of keeping their head, arms and legs inboard when near locks, bridges, tunnels and overhanging trees.
- Do not sit on the cabin roof. (Look out for fish hooks caught in the branches).
- The helmsman should warn the crew when he sees a potential hazard ahead, or if the boat is about to bump into something.

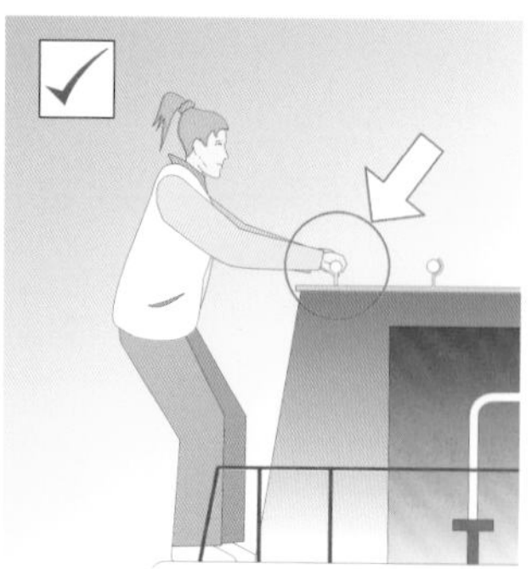

Use the grab rail

- When moving around the outside of the boat, always try to keep one hand for the boat, one hand for you.
- Keep boat poles away from the grab rail so you don't grab the pole by mistake.
- It is sensible to walk through the boat whenever possible.

Walk - don't run

- Surfaces can be wet and slippery – especially around locks.

Use fenders

- Never fend off using your arms or legs. The speed and weight of the boat may be greater than you realise and can cause serious injury.
- When coming into moor, have a fender (on a line) ready to cushion the impact.
- Use larger fenders to keep the boat off awkward obstructions - be aware of vulnerable windows and cabin sides.

Don't swim

- Unfortunately, our waterways are occasionally used for illegal dumping. Submerged old bicycles and supermarket trolleys etc, are potential hazards.
- There may be dangerous currents, especially near weirs and locks.
- The water can be very cold, even in summer.
- Water quality may be poor. Don't let your pets drink the water for the same reason.

Don't drink and drive

- As relevant to boats as it is to cars.

Moor up before nightfall

- It can be dangerous to go boating at night.
- Boating after dark is not permitted by hire boat companies.

BOTTLED GAS, USED FOR COOKERS, FRIDGES AND HEATERS, IS PERFECTLY SAFE IF HANDLED CORRECTLY BUT IT CAN BE DANGEROUS IF FUMES ESCAPE.

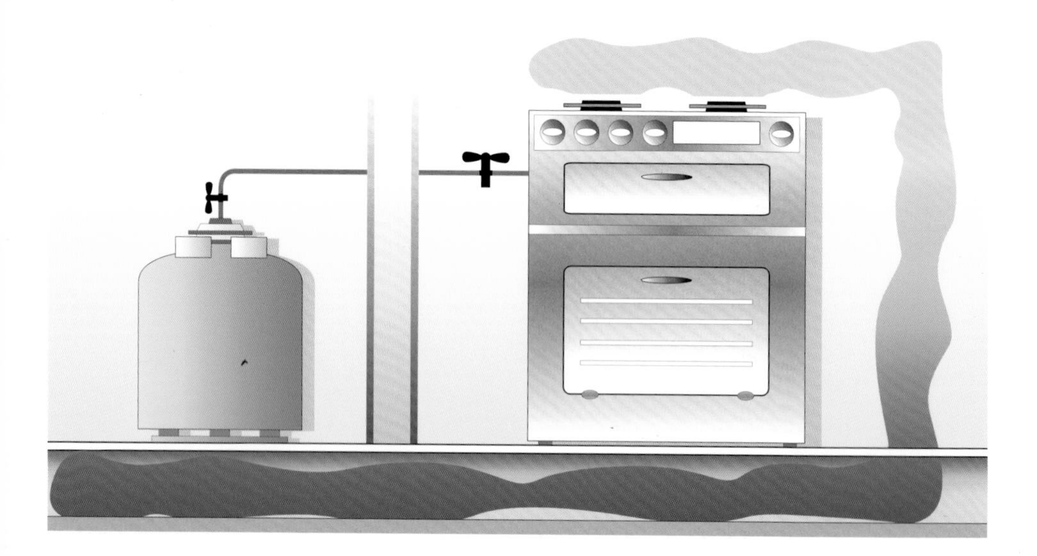

Gas is heavier than air and if there is a leak, it will accumulate in the bilges. It only takes a small spark to ignite.

If you smell gas

1. Get everyone outside.
2. Turn the gas off at source.
3. Ventilate the area.
4. Use a bucket to tip gas over the side.
5. Do not use any electrical switches including bilge pumps, lights, etc, until you are sure that the gas has dispersed.

Sensible precautions

- Switch off all gas appliances when not is use.
- Turn off at the bottle when you leave the boat or go to bed.
- Turn off all gas appliances before you change the gas bottle.
- Store gas bottles in outside lockers which self-drain overboard.
- Do not keep spare gas bottles inside the boat.
- Fit a gas detector and test it regularly.
- Keep ventilators open and clear of obstructions.
- Do not use or store stoves with a portable gas bottle inside the cabin.

ELECTRICITY/SHORE POWER

- Always attach the connection to the boat before plugging into the shore.
- Check your circuit breaker regularly.
- Ensure the lead is not a trip hazard.
- If charging batteries, ensure good ventilation.

VENTILATION

Make sure that exhaust fumes cannot build up inside the boat.

All cooking and heating appliances can produce carbon monoxide if not properly ventilated.

Carbon monoxide poisoning can be a killer. The first signs are headaches, tiredness, sickness and dizziness.

Ensure adequate ventilation throughout the cabin.

BOAT SAFETY SCHEME

Boat Safety

British Waterways and the Environment Agency introduced the Boat Safety Scheme to set boat construction standards and the safe installation of gas and fuel systems, fire extinguishers and much more besides.

All boat owners should comply. The BSS is gradually being adopted by other authorities. Call 01923 201120 for more details

PETROL

- Petrol vapour is explosive.
- Always switch your engine off before refuelling.
- Also turn off all naked lights, such as water heater pilot lights.
- Do not smoke or cook when refuelling.
- Never fill your tank in a lock.
- Do not allow fumes from refuelling to fill the boat – put boat covers up first.
- If there has been a leak, do not start the engine until the spillage has been cleared up.
- If there is petrol or fumes inside the boat, do not start the engine or relight pilot lights until the bilges are clear.
- Fill portable outboard petrol tanks away from the boat.
- Ensure that hose connections are sound and leak free.

DIESEL

Many inland craft have diesel engines which are more economical and less hazardous than petrol.

- Take care not to spill when refuelling.
- Keep the tank vents clear.
- Do not fill with fuel at the same time as you are filling with water.

PRECAUTIONS

- Make sure that the crew know where fire extinguishers and fire blankets are kept, and how to use them.
- Plan your escape route and keep it clear.
- Fit a smoke alarm.
- Don't use a BBQ on the boat.

If you have a fire on board

- First, get the boat to a bank.
- Evacuate the crew to a safe location.
- Call the Fire Services if necessary.

Fire blankets are useful for small galley fires. Hold like this to protect your hands.

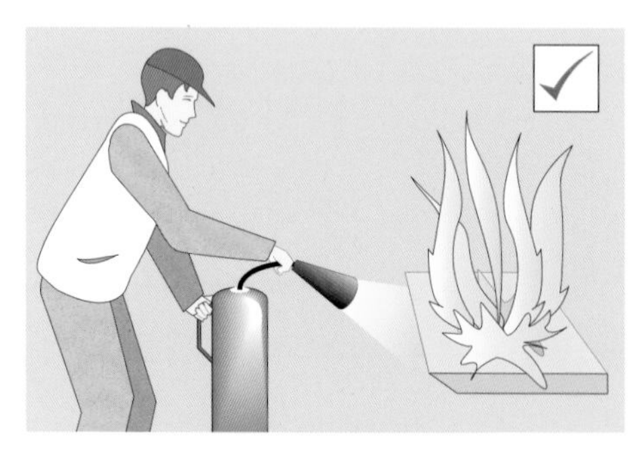

Use of a fire extinguisher

- Keep the extinguisher upright.
- Aim at the base of the fire.
- If the fire is in the engine compartment, only open the lid as far as you have to.
- Do not breathe the smoke - burning plastic is poisonous.

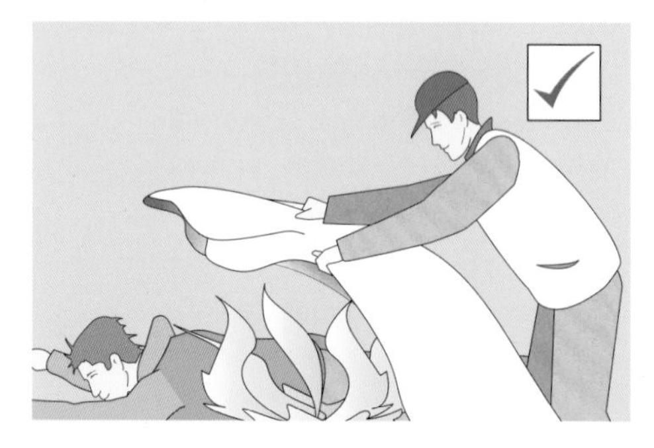

If someone's clothing is alight

- Place him face down so that the flames rise away from his face.
- Smother the flames with a fire blanket or wet jacket/blanket.

Do not use water on fires involving oil, diesel, petrol or electrics.

WASTE DISPOSAL

It is illegal to discharge toilets into the waterway but there are plenty of pump-out stations at locks, boatyards and marinas (details from relevant navigation authorities).

Pump out station.

On British Waterways (BW) navigations you will need a Watermate Key to access the pump out facilities

With a holding tank, make sure that all vents are open before pumping out otherwise the vacuum created could implode the tank.

Waste water from sinks and showers can go straight into the waterway. However, to protect the environment, only use small amounts of biodegradable detergents and soap.

Do not throw any rubbish overboard. Even organic matter can take a long time to rot down and may be harmful to the wild life. Discarded plastic can cause problems for propellers and sluice gates.

Dispose of rubbish where you see this sign.

Don't pump oily water from your boat's bilges into the waterway. Well-maintained engines should not leak oil, but check the drip tray under the engine and gearbox regularly. Use biodegradable oils, if possible.

The British Marine Federation produces an excellent free booklet which explains how you can reduce your impact on the environment.

Call 01784 223600 for a copy.

Report any pollution or fly-tipping to the Environment Agency on.

FREEPHONE 0800 80 70 60

CARE OF THE ENVIRONMENT

Your boat's wash can erode banks, damage plant life and destroy nests and burrows.

If you create a breaking wash, you are going too fast, whatever the speed limit.

The non-towpath side of the canal is often especially rich in flora and fauna.

Do not moor on this side unless there are facilities provided.

Round turn and two half hitches

Ideal for mooring lines as it can be released under tension. Also used for attaching fenders.

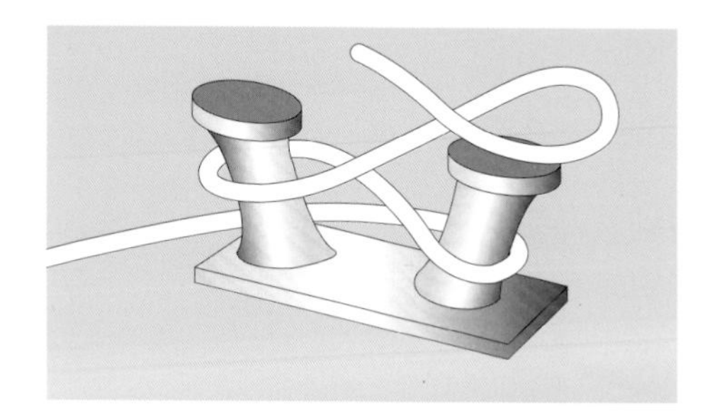

Figure-of-eight

Secure by taking a turn round the back of the cleat, then add two figure-of-eight turns for friction.

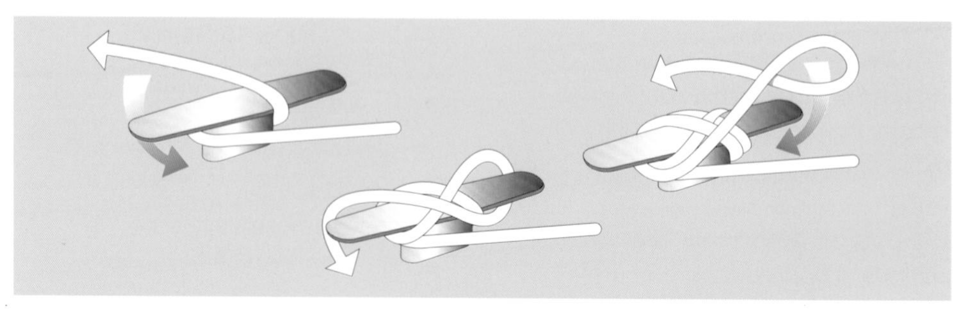

Locking hitch

Take a turn, then make two figure-of-eights over the tee. Finally, make a loop and secure over the horn of the cleat.

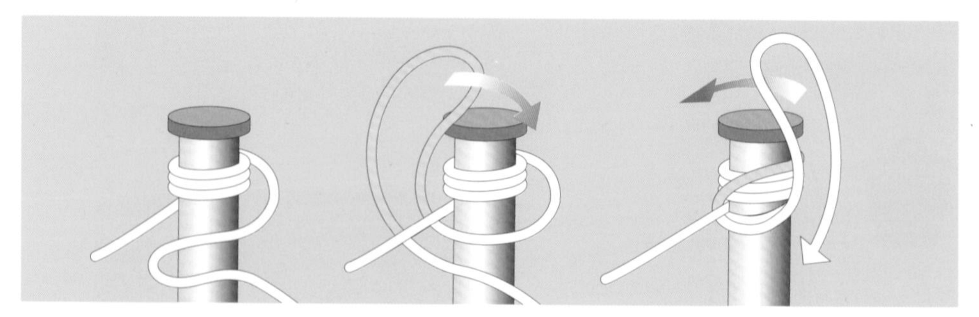

Canalman's hitch

Again, ideal for tying up to cleats or mooring bollards as it can be undone under load. Don't put too many hitches on.

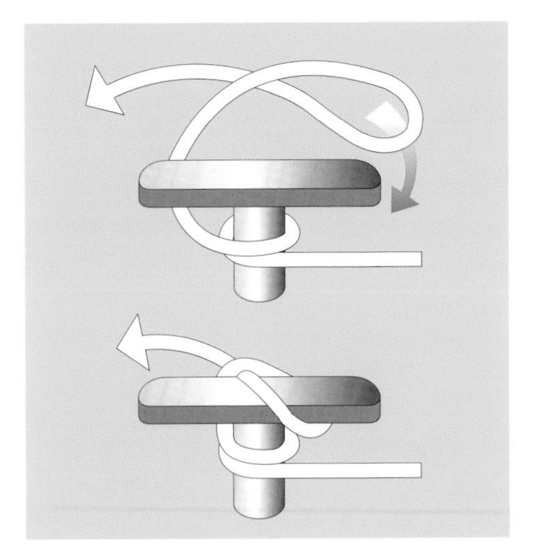

Tee stud hitch

An ideal knot to use with a traditional tee stud. Useful when swigging (opposite). You can loosen the hitch quickly by pushing it off the tee with your foot.

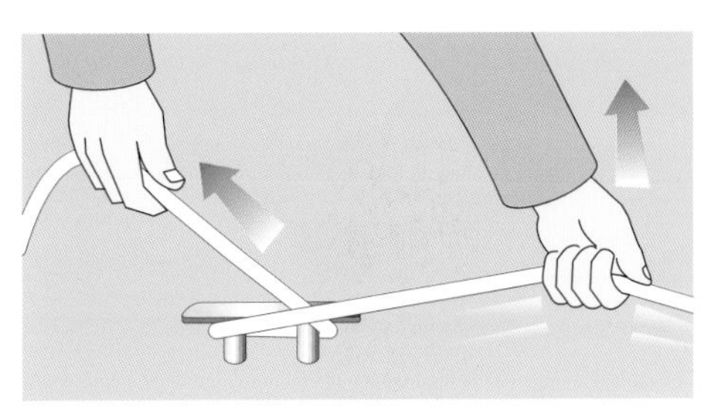

Swigging or Swaging

With a turn around a cleat, you can tighten (or shorten) the line by pulling on the line whilst holding tension on the cleat, then releasing the line whilst taking up the slack.

For heavier applications, use your body weight – but hold on tightly. Never shorten the line by taking turns over the cleat or tee stud. When it is untied, it will jam.

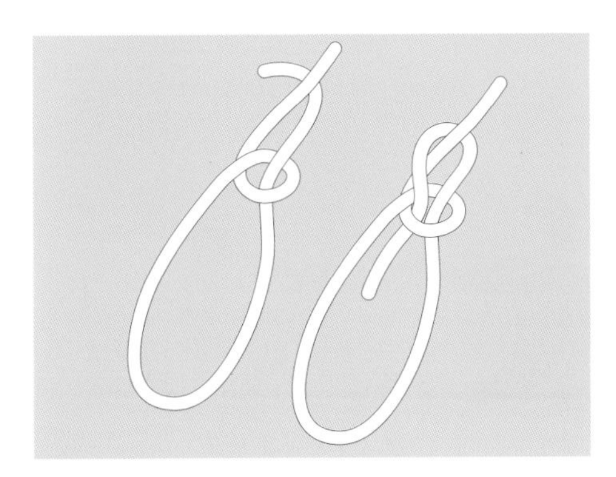

Bowline

Ideal for making a loop to put over a bollard or used as a rescue aid *(see p33)*
Cannot be undone under load.

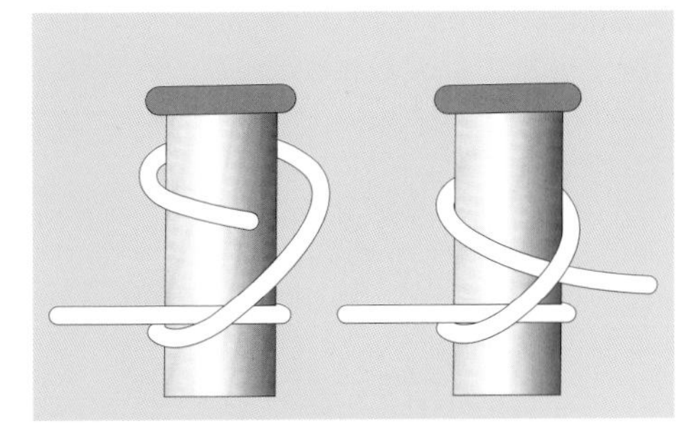

Clove hitch

Easy way to attach a line to a round handrail. Essential when using mooring stakes: if the stake goes into the water, the line will stay attached, making it easy to recover.

Handling lines

To join two lines together, use a double sheet bend. Ideal for different diameter ropes.

Coiling a line

A regular rhythm of an arm's length creates an even coil. Three strand (laid) rope is coiled clockwise with a right hand twist in each turn. Plaited rope tends to form figure-of-eights.

Both can be stored like this. Always keep lines tidy.

Throwing a line

Coil the line and divide it in two. Swing and throw the end coil while releasing the other. Make sure one end is secure otherwise you will throw the whole line.

Twin coil throw

Make one end fast around a cleat. Divide the rope into two coils and using both hands, throw the line forward over the bollard so that the line forms a large loop. Then pull in slack.

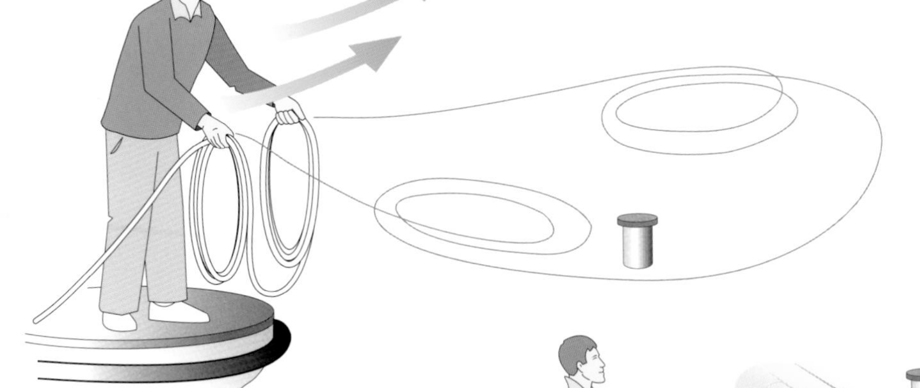

Taking the strain

Take the load by making a half turn round the tee stud or cleat. Ideal in a lock as you can surge the line in or out to control the boat: pull to apply friction, ease to release.

Don't take a full turn round the tee stud in this situation – if you do it could jam as your boat descends.

Flick the line to release the eye splice from the bollard.

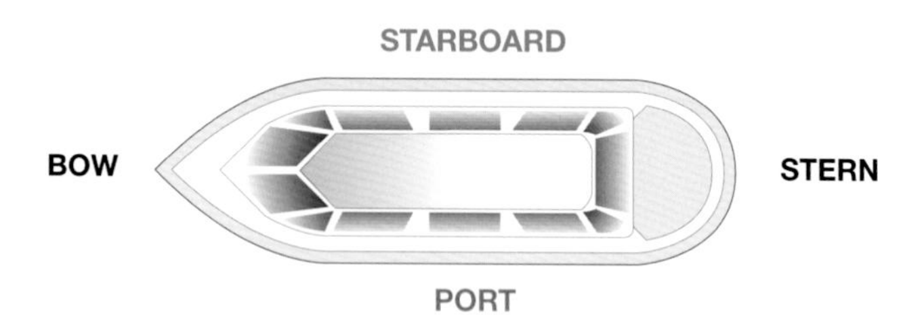

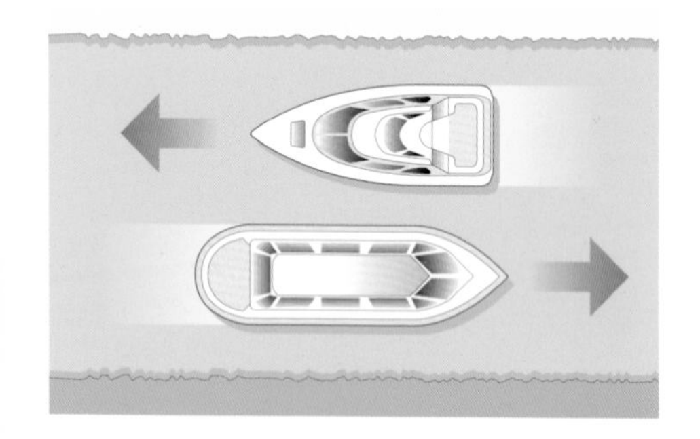

Keep to the right when passing approaching craft. Port-to-port (left-to-left) is the general rule on all waterways.

Overtake on the left. Don't overtake near bridges or bends. Make sure that the other boat knows your intentions.

If you are overtaking it's your responsibility to keep clear of the other boat.

If you are the overtaken boat, it is polite to slow down to allow the other boat to pass.

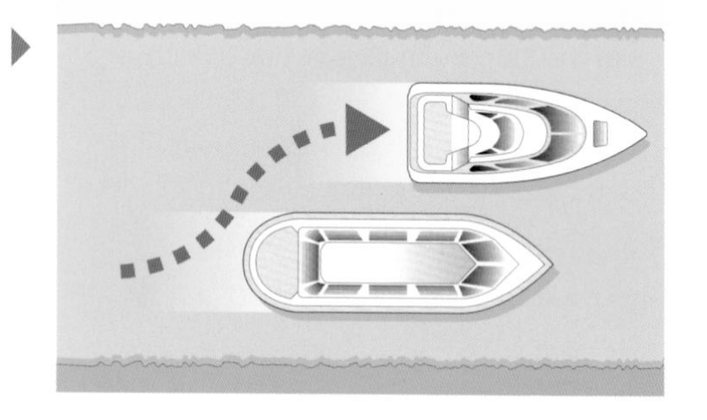

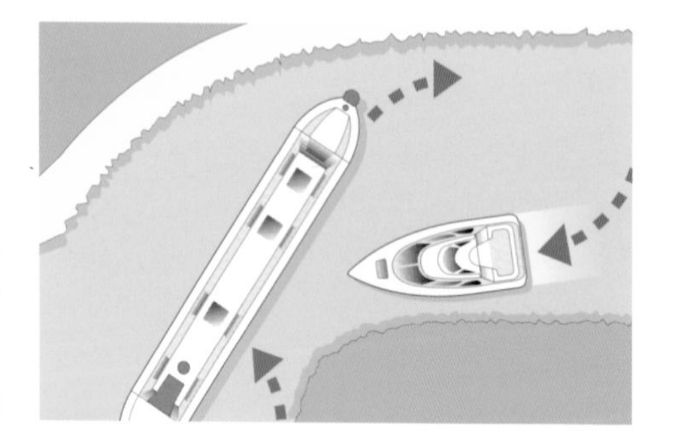

Large boats may need to swing wide on bends. Wait if you can or sound two short blasts 'I am turning to port' *(see p65)* and pass on the wrong side.

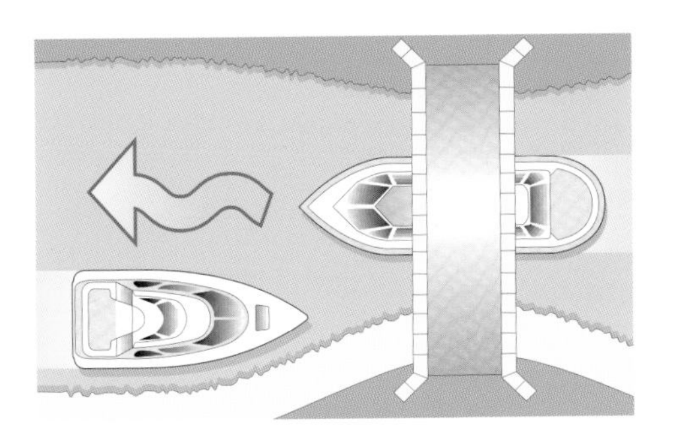

When approaching a bridge or other narrow section, slow down well in advance.

If a boat coming the other way is nearer, wave them through first.
Keep right until they are clear.

On rivers, the boat coming downstream has right of way.

The navigation channel on a river is marked by buoys:

Facing upstream:	**RED** buoys (can) are on the left. **GREEN** buoys (cone) are on the right.
Facing downstream:	**RED** buoys are on the right. **GREEN** buoys are on the left.

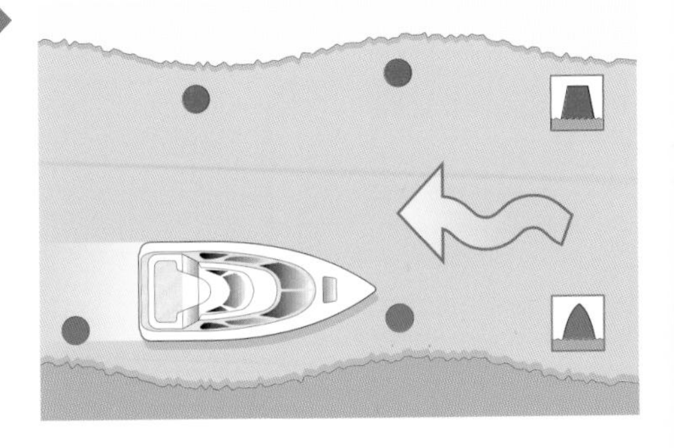

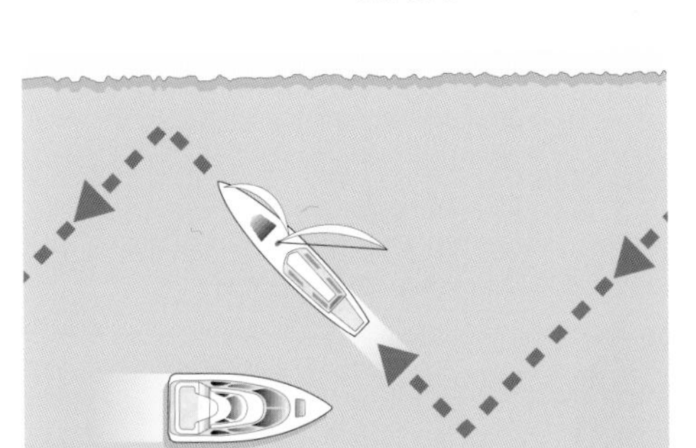

Sailing boats often need to zig zag (tack) to make progress against the wind.

When approaching a sailing boat, slow down and wait for an opportunity to pass astern.

Never cross in front unless you are asked to do so.

If you get caught up in a boat race, slow down but maintain your course.

Wide rivers often have strong currents especially midstream and on the outside of bends. Boats going upstream can stay close to the edge or the inside of bends where the current is weaker but it may be shallower.

Rowing boats may be using the current to their advantage. As rowers may not see you, use sound signals to show your intentions (see p65).
On some waters they have right of way.

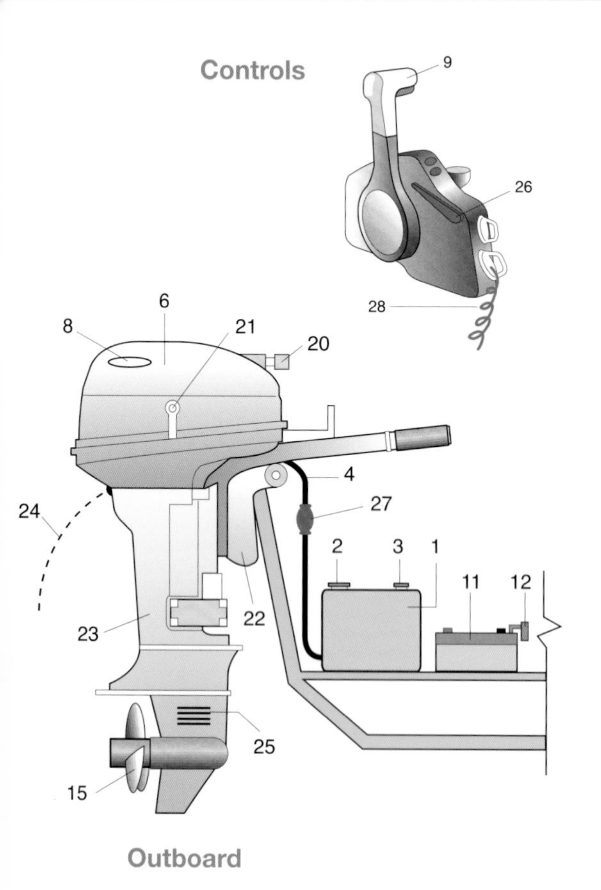

1 fuel tank
2 fuel filler
3 fuel tank vent
4 fuel line
5 fuel filters
6 engine
7 oil dipstick
8 oil filler
9 single lever control
10 cooling water header tank
11 starter battery
12 battery isolater switch
13 stern tube greaser
14 weed hatch
15 propeller
16 gearbox dipstick
17 cooling water intake filter
18 keel cooler
19 stern tube
20 engine hand start
21 gear operating lever
22 transom mounting bracket
23 outboard / outdrive leg
24 cooling water tell tale
25 cooling water inlet grille
26 fast idle control (some controls only)
27 fuel bulb
28 kill cord (always attach this to yourself when engine is running)

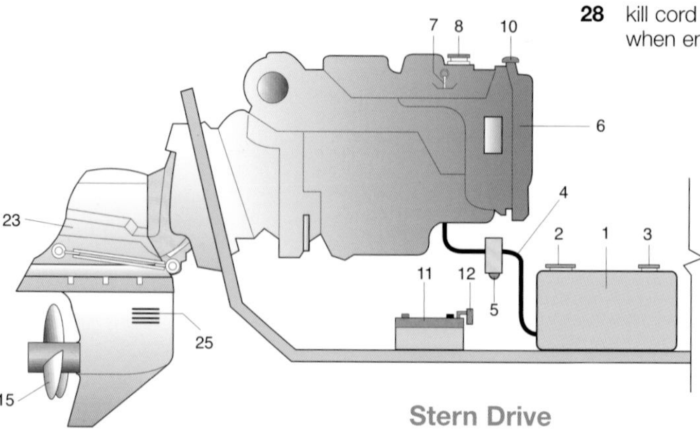

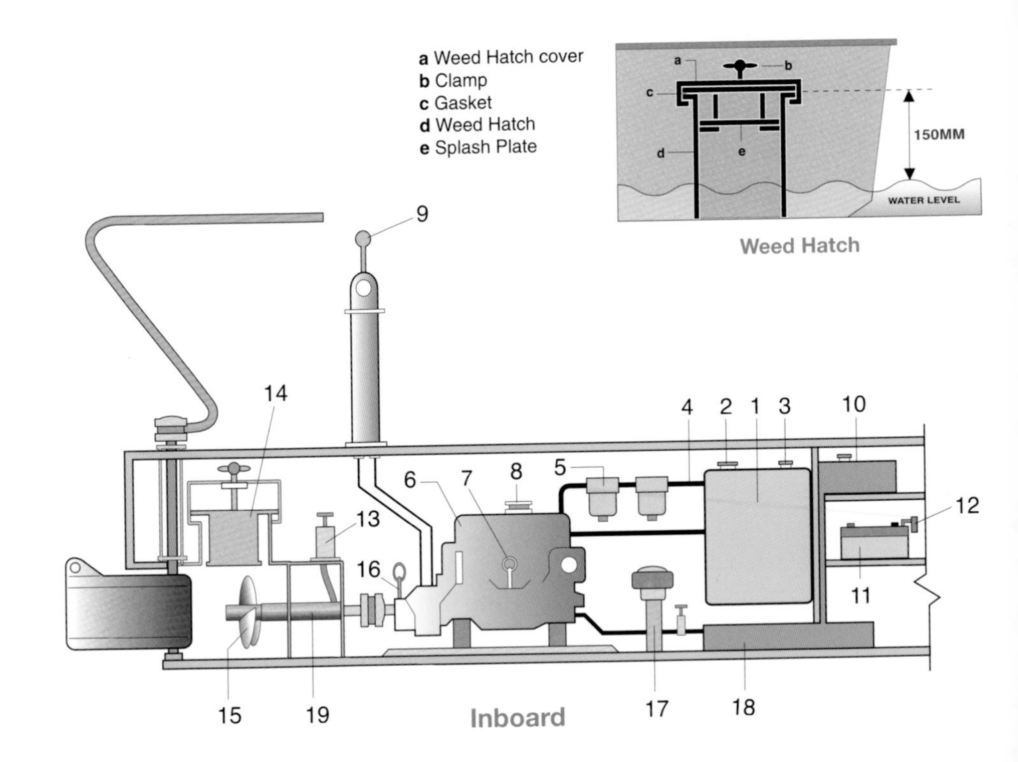

Pre-start checks.

For both types

- Ensure engine is in neutral
- Check fuel level & fuel turned to on
- Turn battery isolator on
- Check engine gearbox oil levels
- Check any drive belts for condition and tension
- Ensure air vent on tank is open

For Diesel

- Check stern tube for leaks and use greaser
- Check header tank level
- Check cooling water filters
- Ensure engine stop is returned
- Turn key and hold for a few seconds until the engine starts

For Petrol

- If inboard vent engine bay of any fumes before starting
- Prime fuel system by squeezing bulb
- Engage choke (if needed)
- Some engines require some revs in neutral
- Electric start, use starter in short burst
- Manual start make sure other crew are clear then give a good solid pull on the cord
- When started check cooling water tell tale
- Return choke knob if used
- Adjust throttle to allow for warm up

ALL BOATS HAVE DIFFERENT HANDLING CHARACTERISTICS SO PRACTISE IS THE BEST WAY TO GET TO KNOW YOUR BOAT.

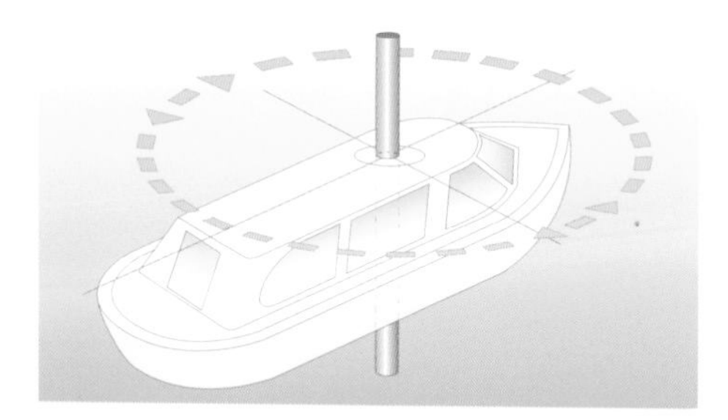

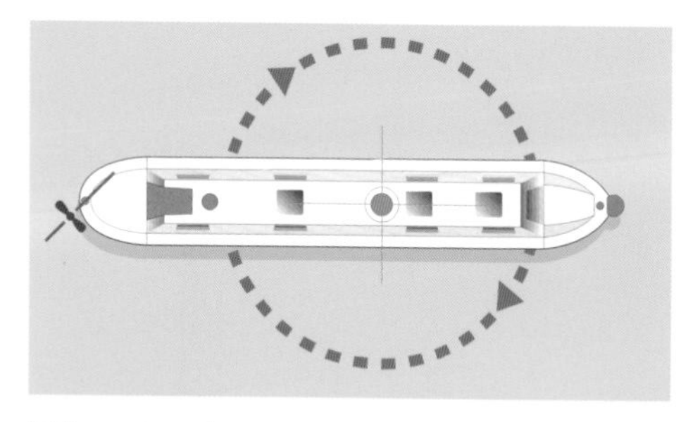

Pivot point

Boats don't steer like cars. Going forwards, they pivot on a point about one third to half way from the bow so allow enough room for the stern to move sideways when turning. (much like a shopping trolley).

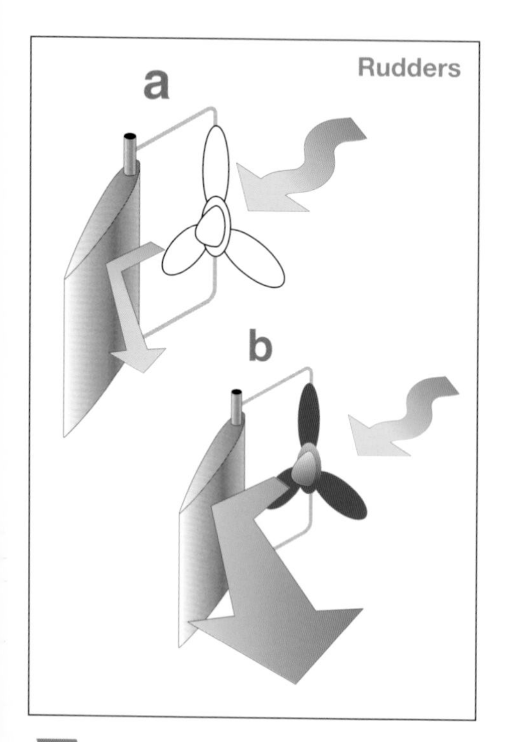

Tiller steering

Push the tiller away from the direction you want to go. Tiller steering from the stern allows you to judge the swing of the bow and position the stern more easily. On most narrowboats, if the engine is in neutral you will not be able to steer.

Wheel steering

Turn the wheel in the direction you want to go. Wheel steering is less direct than a tiller and when the wheel is at the front of the boat it is difficult to see what the stern is doing.

Rudders

a The rudder works by deflecting the water passing over the surface.
On most narrow-boats the rudder has little effect when coasting along in neutral. The same is true for outdrive boats. Some cruisers answer the helm quite well out of gear. Generally the rule is ***No Gear = No Steer.***

b When the prop is in forward gear, water passes over the rudder's surface so the boat will steer better. In confined spaces, a short bust of power will increase the rudder's effect without imparting too much additionally momentum.

WHEN MANOEUVRING IN CONFINED SPACES, A SHORT BURST OF POWER WILL INCREASE STEERAGE WITHOUT ADDING TOO MUCH SPEED.

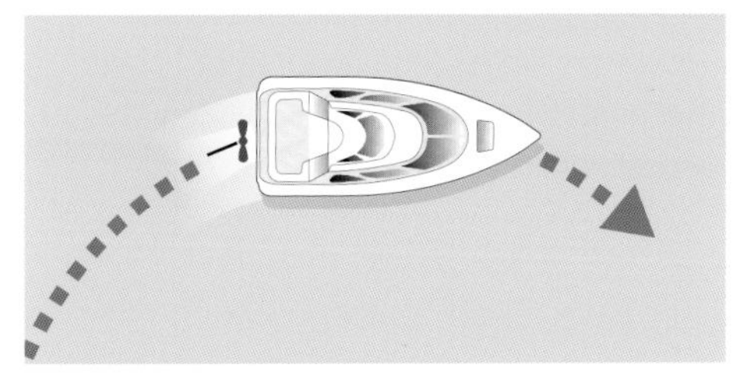

At low revs, the boat will turn slowly in a large arc.

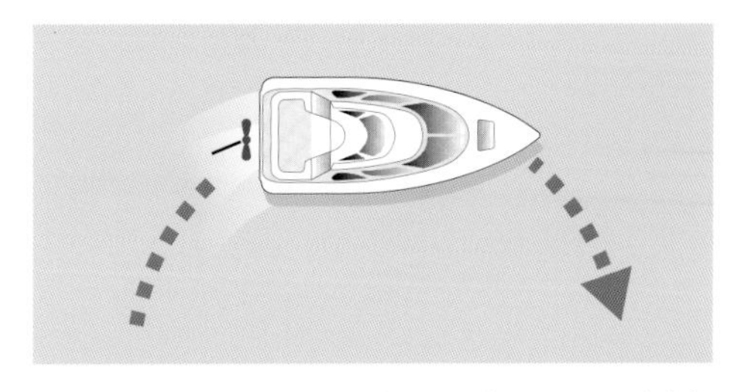

By increasing the revs, the boat will turn more tightly but more quickly.

On narrow boats, 'pumping' the tiller will help you turn in confined spaces.
Many boats will slip sideways during a turn. This is aggravated by a crosswind.

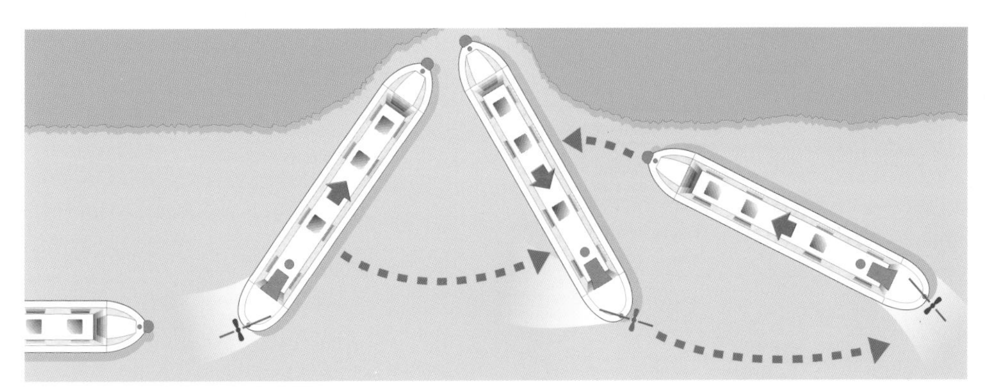

Turning in a winding hole

On canals or narrow rivers, longer boats will need to use a winding hole.

- Always put the bow into the winding hole never the stern, otherwise you will damage the prop.
- Push the tiller over and start turning into the winding hole.
- Glide gently up to the deepest part, applying reverse to stop with the bows resting gently on the bank.
- Now apply revs in forward gear with the tiller pointing the way you want to go.
- The stern will motor across to the other side of the winding hole.
- Push the tiller the other way and reverse off until you are clear. As before, if you can use prop effect it will help you turn. *(see p37)*.

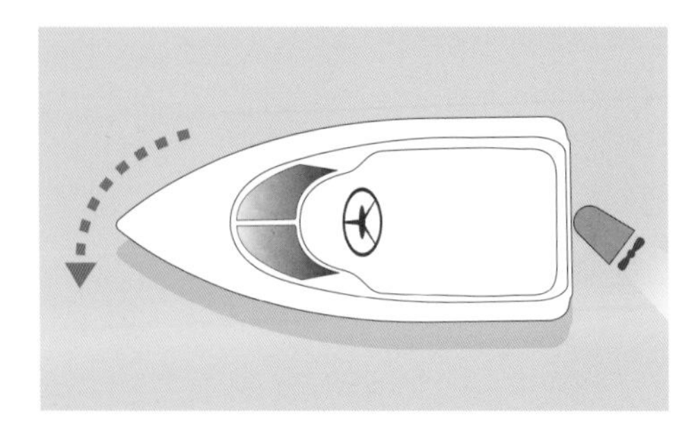

Outboards

Although some outboards have an add-on rudder to improve slow speed manoeuvring, most can only steer the boat when the propeller is driving.

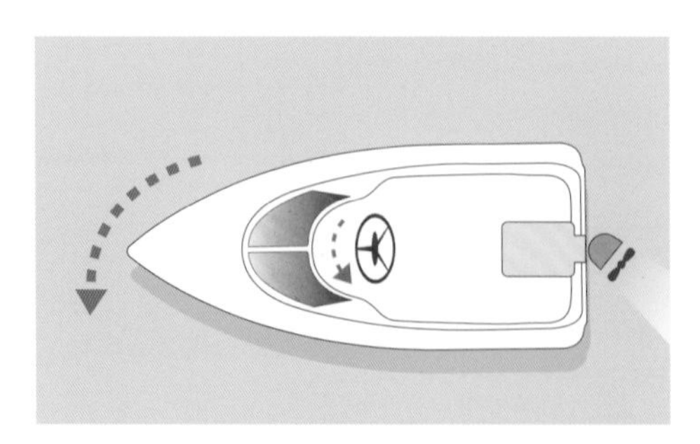

Outdrives and sterndrives

These steer like an outboard but the engine is inside the boat. Much sharper turns can be achieved in both directions than with a conventional prop and rudder system.

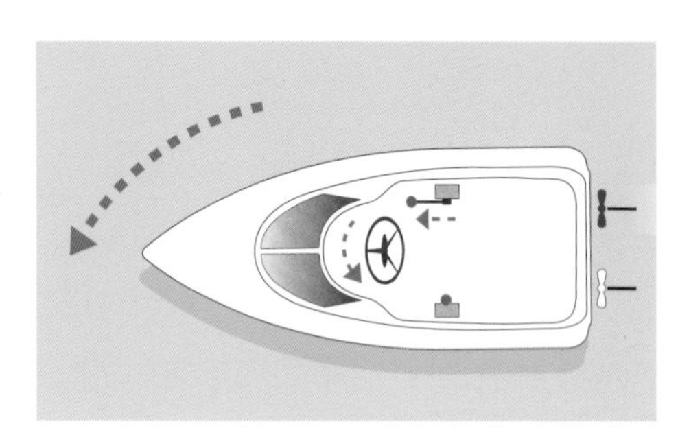

Twin outdrives

With twin outdrives the outside one will have greater leverage then the inside one.

So, to turn left: wheel to the left and power on right engine. Opposite to turn right.

Outboards, outdrives and sterndrives all have a common theme:

- Engine to neutral / steer the leg / apply the power
- This gives maximum manoeuvrability / minimum speed.

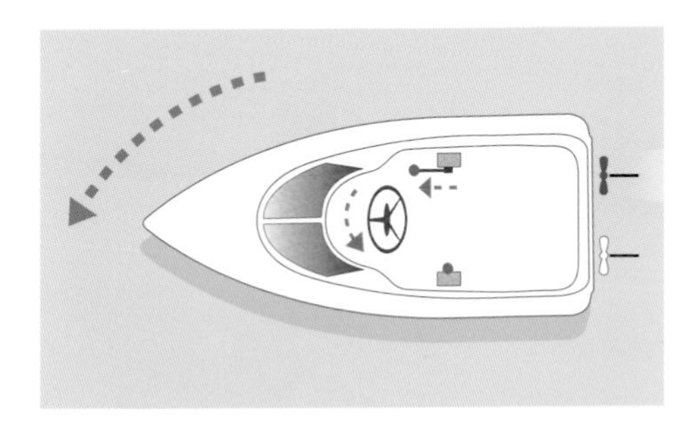

Twin props

As the propellers are offset from the centre line of the boat, by running just one you can turn the boat without using the rudders.

To make a tighter turn, use the rudders as well.

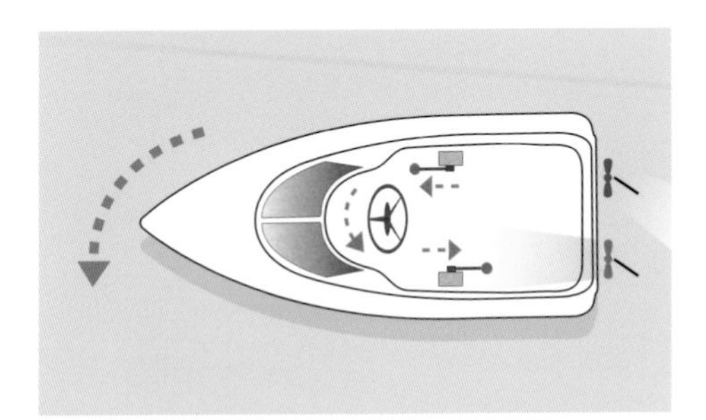

For a really tight turn, put the rudders hard over and go ahead on one engine and astern with the other. The combined effect will turn the boat in her own length.

Use power in short bursts (tickover is often sufficient) to stop speed and momentum building up.

MOST INLAND WATERWAY BOATS DO NOT STEER WELL IN REVERSE SO IT TAKES PRACTISE.

Tiller steering

- Make allowances for the wind.
- On narrow canals, keep the boat in the centre of the channel.
- Once central, look astern and point the rudder in the direction you want to go.
- Keep looking forward to check the swing of the bow. The pivot point is further back in reverse.
- If the bow is swinging the wrong way, point the rudder in the opposite direction to correct it.

Wheel steering

- Look astern and turn the wheel in the direction you want the stern to go. Continually check the bow swing and alter the wheel position accordingly.
- Use as little power as possible.
- Use neutral to stop momentum building up.

On twin engine boats, use alternate engines to keep the speed down.

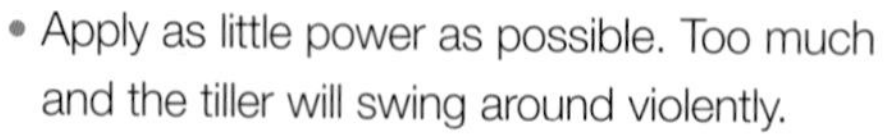

- Apply as little power as possible. Too much and the tiller will swing around violently.
- If you have a bow thruster use in short bursts only.

On canals

- If someone falls overboard, think before you act. Don't jump in yourself or let anyone else do so.
- Put the engine into neutral to stop the prop.

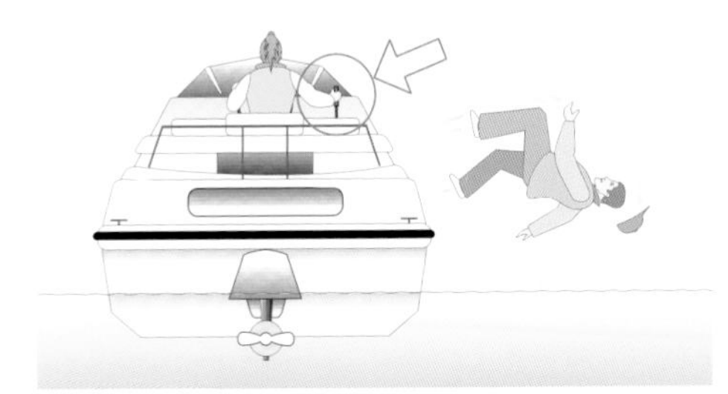

- Do not reverse back to the MOB, they could get sucked into the prop.
- Throw a lifebelt to the MOB.

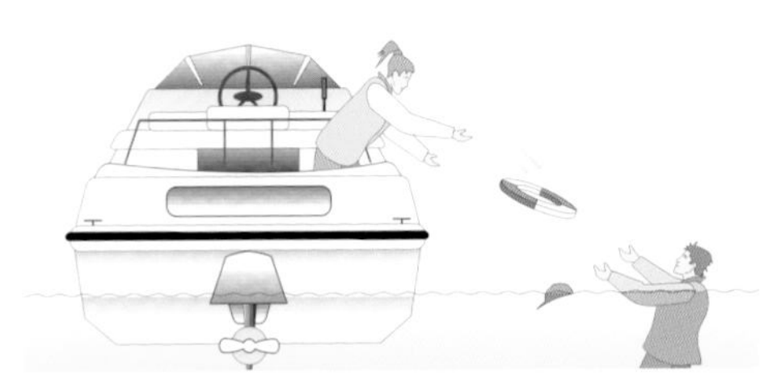

- Tell them to try and stand up. Canals are quite shallow, especially at the edges, so they may be able to wade to the bank.
- Head the boat for the bank and get someone off the boat to help the MOB climb out of the water.

On wide rivers and deeper canals

If the MOB cannot stand up:

- Throw a lifebelt to the MOB.
- Proceed past the MOB, keeping the boat's stern well away from them.
- Turn the boat round and approach the MOB very slowly up into the current.

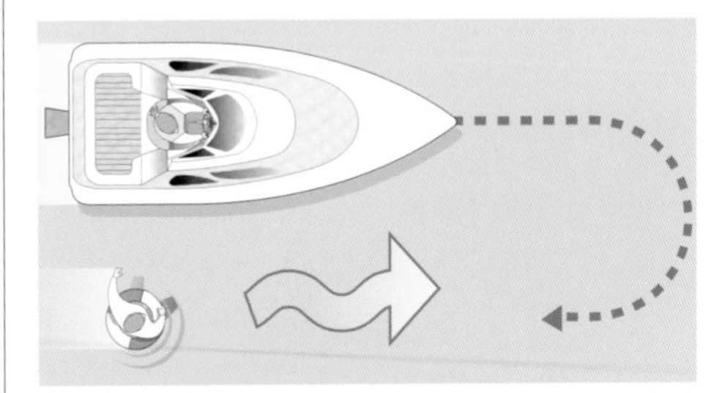

- Put the engine in neutral. You and the MOB will both drift at the same speed on a river.

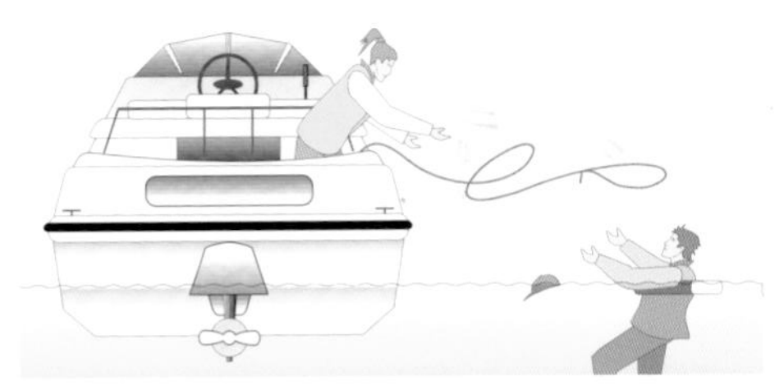

- Throw the MOB a line with a large bowline at the end *(see p21)*.
- Tell the MOB to put the rope over his head and under his armpits.
- Pull the MOB to the side of the boat and help them aboard.

In any MOB situation you need to act quickly. If you go through the drill with the crew before you set off, everyone will know what to do and when. Make sure that all the crew know where the safety equipment is kept and know how to use it.

Although the risk of infection is small, it is sensible to take the following precautions after falling in:
• Take a shower • Wash all cuts and abrasions and treat with a sterile dressing • Wash wet clothing thoroughly before further use • If flu-like symptoms develop within two weeks, see a doctor. Tell him that you fell in the canal/river.

Boats do not have brakes and will travel quite a long way after you take the engine out of gear. Even if you go into reverse, the momentum will still carry the boat forward for a while. So slow down early, ease off the throttle to tick over in forward gear and only use reverse to come to a final stop. Remember, many boats don't steer well in neutral.

Bank effect

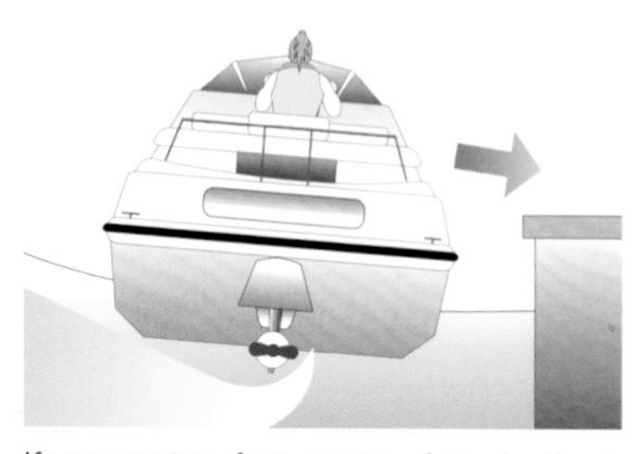

If you go too fast or too close to the bank or another boat, the water between you gets displaced and the boat(s) are sucked sideways. This can seriously affect your steering so anticipate it happening.

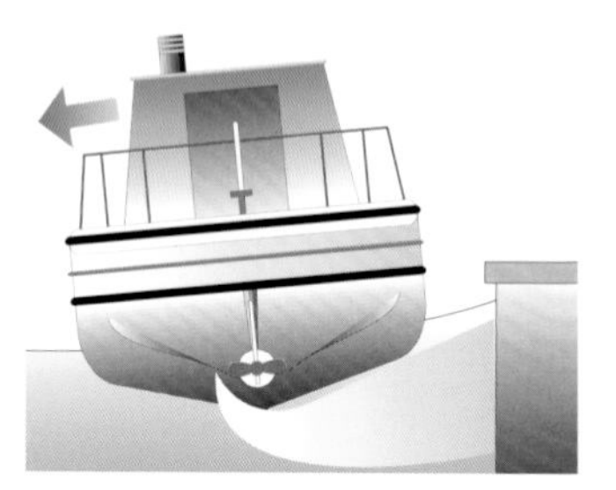

Going in reverse, due to the underwater shape of a narrowboat the prop-wash can get pushed down between the hull and the bank, forcing the stern out.

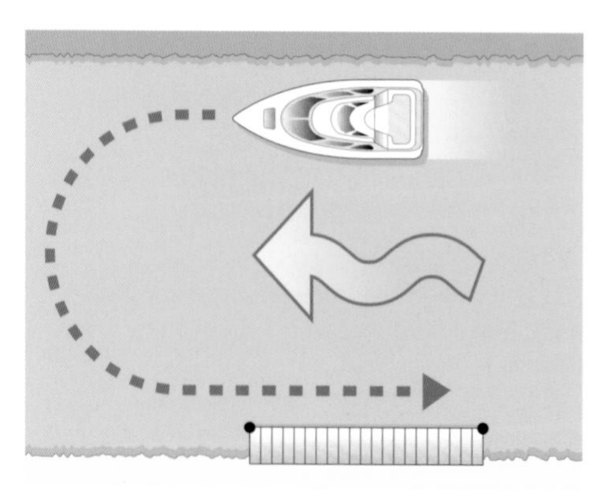

Using the current to help you stop

It is much easier to stop by turning around and heading into the current. It is also easier to moor this way round. Plus, your propeller(s) will not be fouled by debris floating downstream.

Always look behind you before turning to check that the way is clear - use correct sound signals *(see p65)*.

Allow plenty of room if turning downstream. The current may carry you further than you anticipate. Note: currents can speed up dramatically near weirs and bridges.
Be cautious turning upstream of bridges.

Speed over ground

On rivers, the current will affect your speed over the ground.

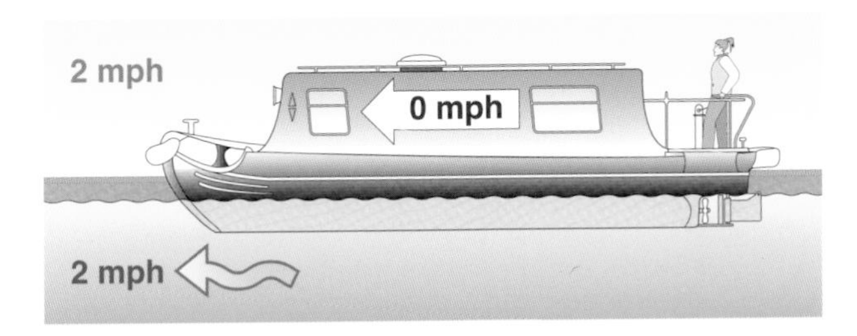

Going downstream, even with no power, you will travel at the current's speed of 2 mph.

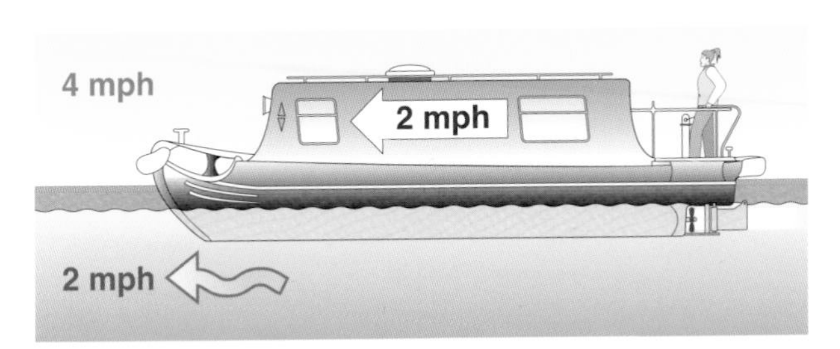

With the engine pushing the boat through the water at 2 mph plus the current's speed of 2 mph you will be moving at a combined speed of 4 mph.

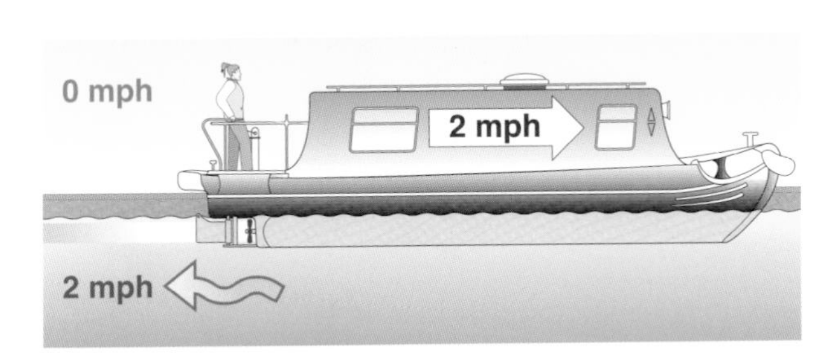

Heading upstream, the boat will need to make 2 mph through the water just to stand still against the 2 mph current.

STRONG CURRENTS

Although canals are normally pond-like, rivers may have strong currents. This can make boat handling interesting and good judgement is required.

- Make sure that your boat has enough power to cope with the flow of the river. If not, tie up and wait for a change in the strength of the current.
- Keep an anchor and chain handy in the upstream end of the boat.
- Check local information and obey warning signs.
- Keep well clear of weirs – watch out for warning signs.

CROSSWINDS CAN HAVE A SERIOUS EFFECT, SO ALWAYS BE AWARE OF WHERE THE WIND IS COMING FROM.

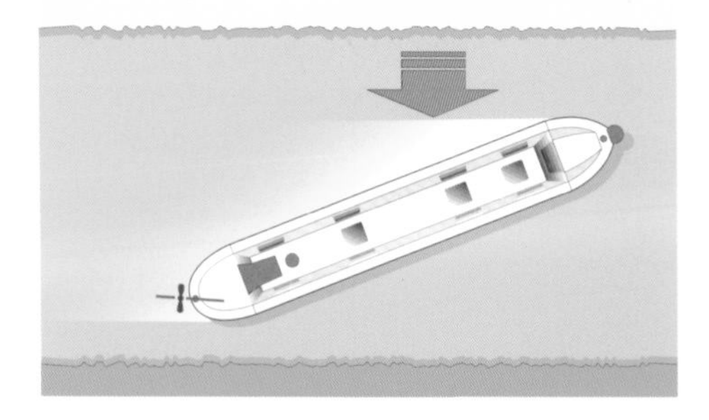

If there is a crosswind, adopt a 'crab-like' position, steering the bow into the wind.

The stronger the crosswind, the greater the angle.

Keep the stern in deep water to gain maximum push from the prop.

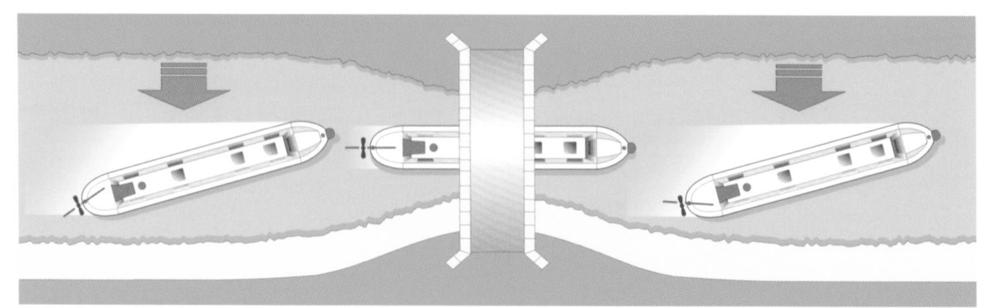

Straighten up to go through bridges. Once through, increase the engine revs and resume the 'crab' position as soon as possible.

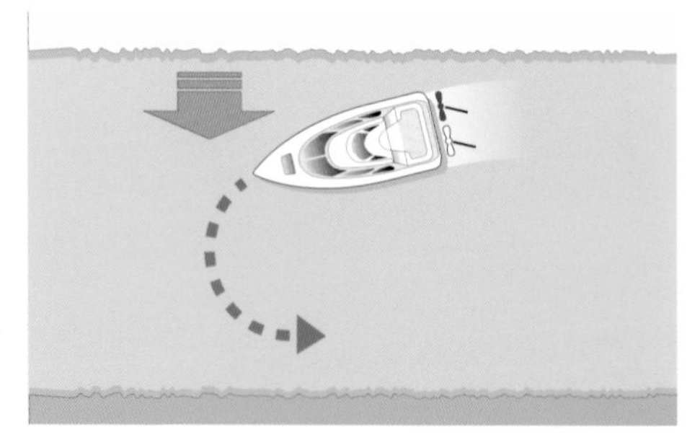

Use the wind to help you turn round. Turning away from the wind (downwind) can help to push the bow round on some boats.

On a narrowboat, however, it may just push you sideways so turn into the wind if possible.

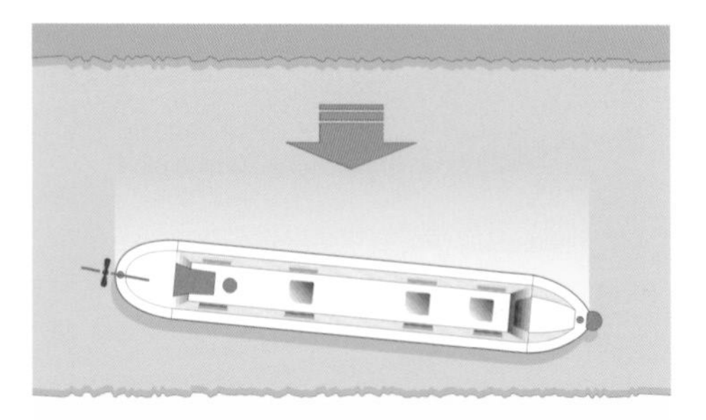

You can harness a crosswind to gently push you onto or off the bank. However, be aware of sudden gusts of wind.

You can see the wind by ripples on the water, flying flags, moving trees and bushes.

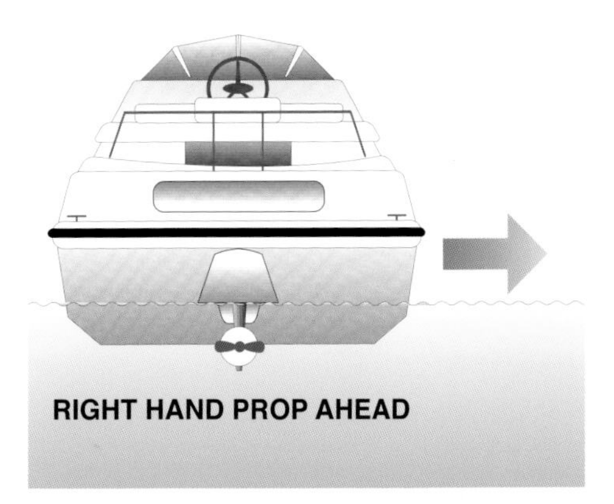

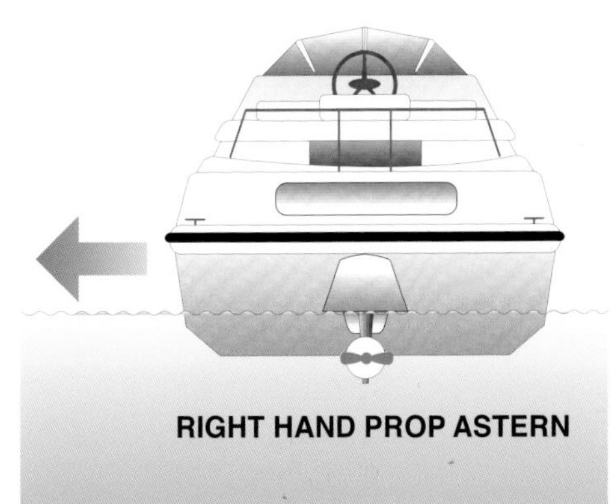

Paddlewheel effect

A right-handed propeller rotates clockwise when ahead gear is engaged, pushing the stern to starboard, and anti-clockwise in astern, pushing the stern to port; vice versa for the left-handed propeller.

Think of the propeller as a rolling wheel. In most cases, paddlewheel effect is only significant for a few seconds after you engage gear, until the boat starts to move through the water.

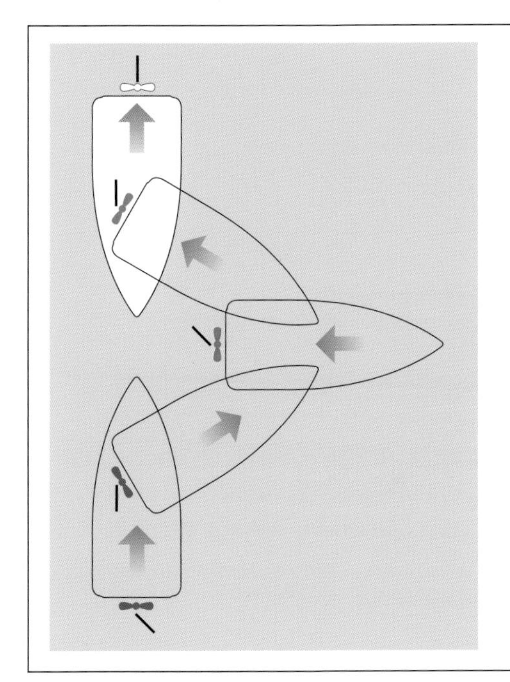

Ideal three-point turn

If the boat has a right-handed propeller, the stern will kick to port when you go astern, giving you much more help than the rudder.

- In a very narrow channel you might have to go ahead and astern several times.
- The secret of tight turning is always to put the wheel hard over before engaging gear.

Turning 180 degrees

Choose your turning direction to take advantage of prop effect, wind and current.

- Put the helm over, burst of revs ahead to start the turn, into neutral.
- Then apply opposite helm and give a burst astern to keep her turning with prop effect, into neutral.
- Apply opposite helm again and go ahead to bring her round.

On all canals the maximum speed is 4 mph (fast walking pace). On shallow waterways you may need to travel much slower. On rivers, where the water is deeper and the channel wider, speed limits vary between 5 - 8mph depending on whether you are going up or downstream. Check local regulations.

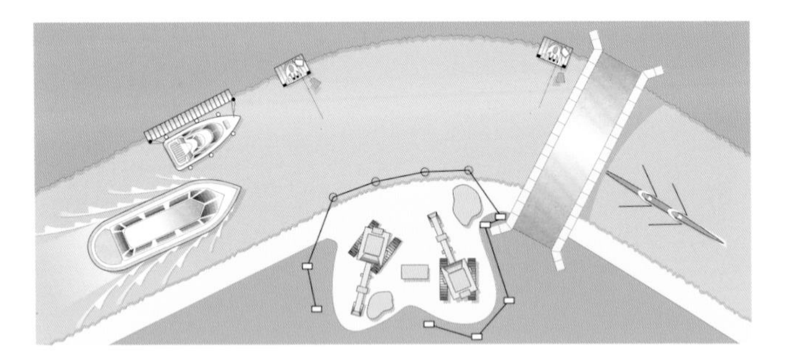

Slow down when:

- You are making a breaking wave along the bank.
- Passing moored craft, rowers or anglers.
- Passing engineering works. Look for which side to pass - green or white markers.
- Negotiating blind bends.
- Passing through narrow bridges, over aqueducts, entering tunnels or anywhere else with a channel restriction.
- If in doubt, slow down, or stop, and assess the situation before proceeding.

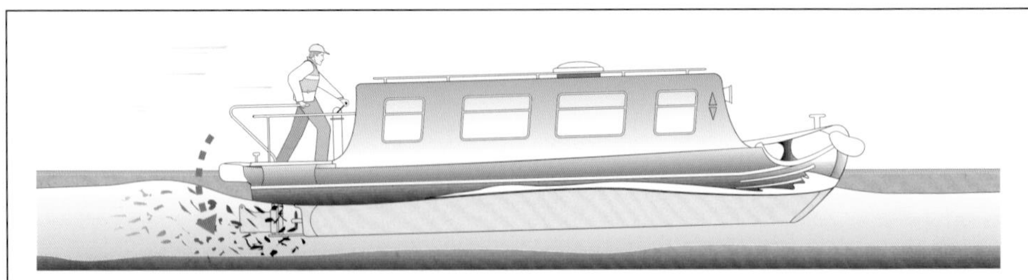

In shallow water you probably won't go any faster by opening up the throttle. All this will do is suck the stern down and disturb bottom debris, which can damage the prop.

You may encounter all sorts of floating rubbish, especially under bridges. As you approach, speed up and then reduce to tick over (or neutral if it is really bad) and glide through. This way, you will not foul your prop.

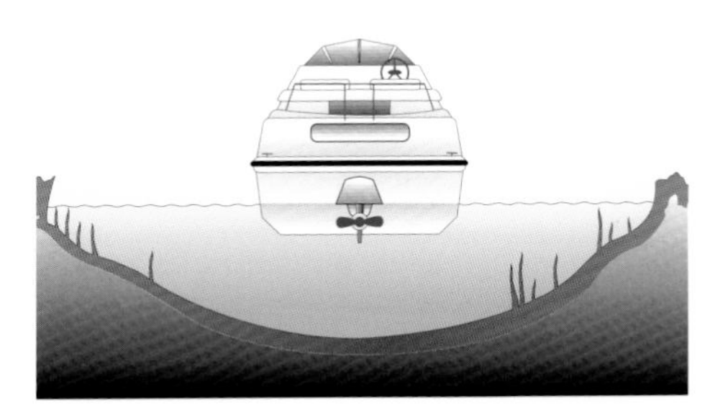

Canals are generally saucer shaped and deeper in the middle.

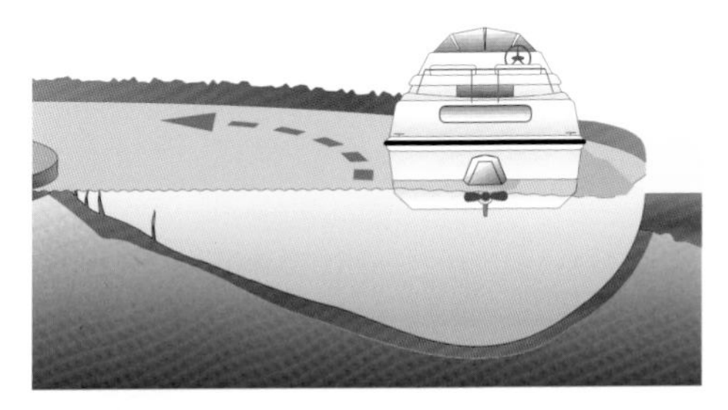

Bends are deeper on the outside where the water has scoured out the channel.

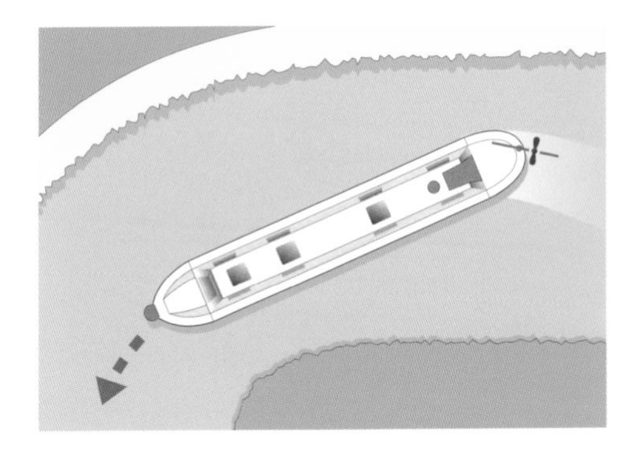

On tight bends you may have to put the helm over and give bursts of forward throttle to get the boat to swing round. Do not cut the corner – or you may run aground.

GOING AGROUND

If you go aground going forwards, you should be able to reverse off.

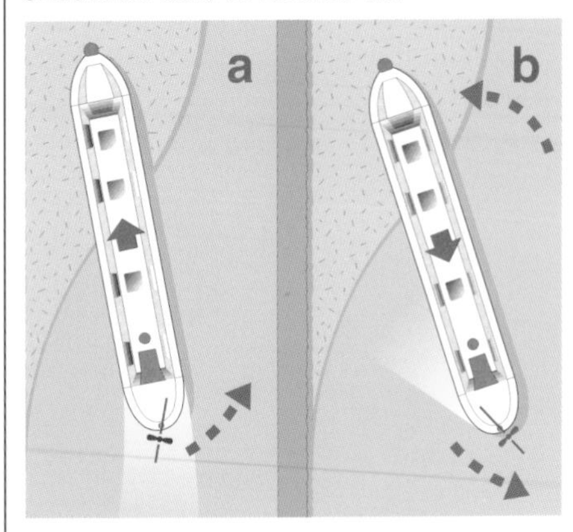

Don't try to turn away from the bank.

(a) First, turn towards the bank to put the stern in deeper water.
(b) Now reverse off.

If that doesn't work, position the crew along the side of the boat away from the shallows and try to reverse again. Rocking the boat sometimes helps.

Use the pole to keep the stern in deep water or to push the fore end off. Place the pole firmly on the bank so it won't slip. Hold the pole to the side of you. Don't use the pole as a lever, it will only break.

As many river banks are privately owned, finding an overnight river mooring can sometimes be a problem. However, there will be public moorings available, usually in riverside towns and villages. Most cruising guides show the public mooring sites.

Popular moorings fill up quickly, so you may need to arrive early to find space or be prepared to double up with other craft.

On canals the situation is easier, mooring along the towpath is normally free for up to 14 days in one place.

The picture illustrates prohibited areas.

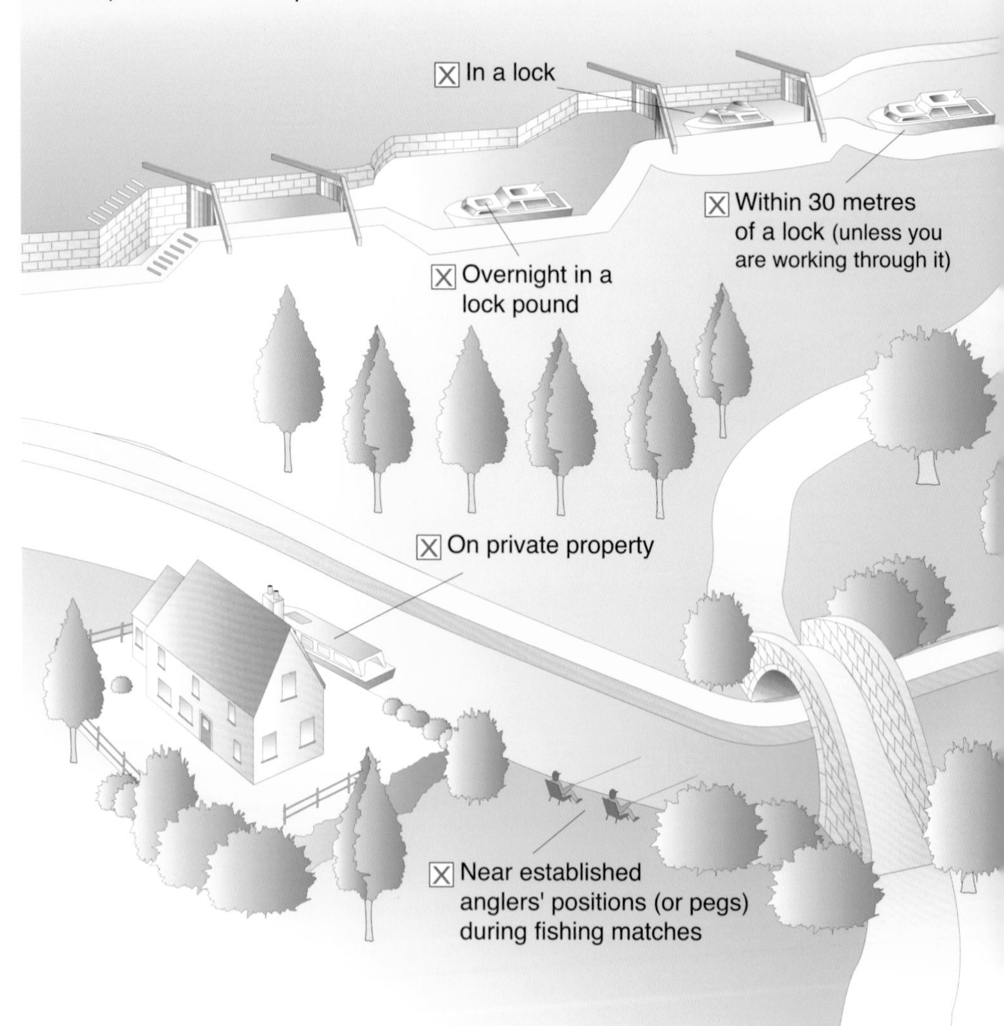

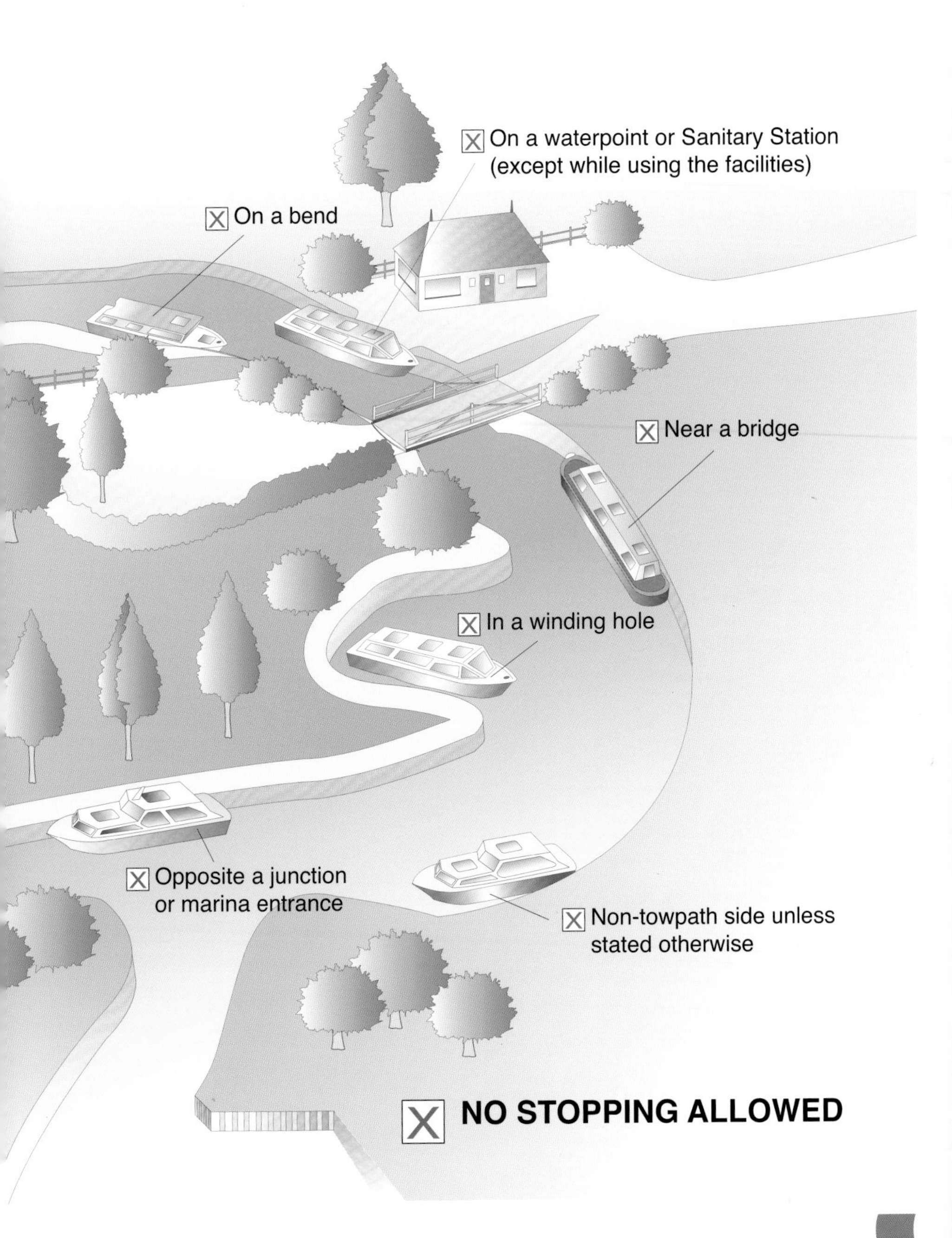
On a waterpoint or Sanitary Station (except while using the facilities)
On a bend
Near a bridge
In a winding hole
Opposite a junction or marina entrance
Non-towpath side unless stated otherwise
NO STOPPING ALLOWED

ON A RIVER, ALWAYS MOOR WITH YOUR BOW FACING UPSTREAM INTO THE CURRENT.

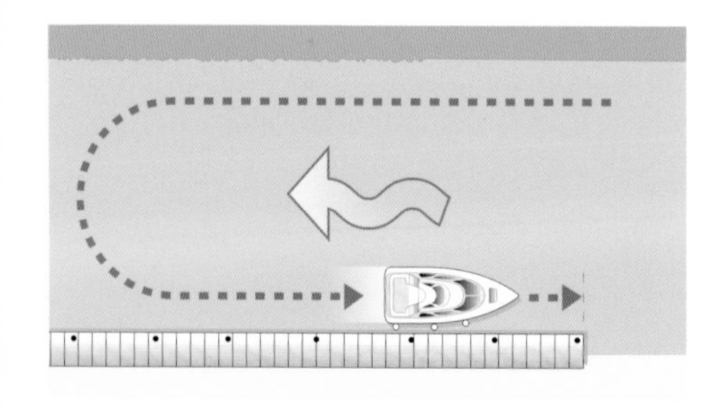

If cruising downstream, you will need to turn your boat:

- Before you turn, brief your crew and have mooring lines and fenders ready.
- Proceed downstream past the mooring, then check that the river is clear of traffic.
- Turn round smartly into the current *(see p34)*.
- Move upstream to the pontoon, stopping at the top end (to allow others to moor behind you).

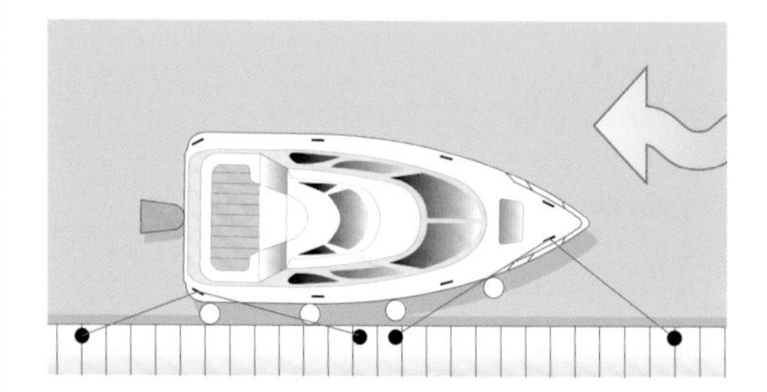

- Secure the bow first, then the stern line
- Position the fenders in the correct place.
- Use spring lines if the boat is surging back and forth in the current or the wash of other boats.
- If you are mooring on a river overnight, leave some slack in the mooring lines to allow for a fall or rise in the water level.
- If you are mooring on a tidal river, make sure you will have enough water at low tide.

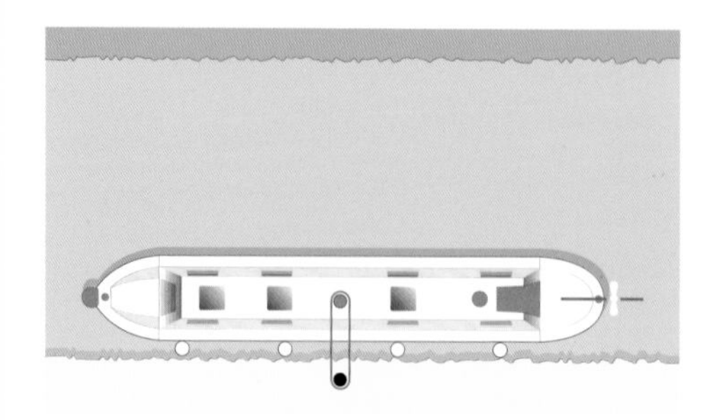

- A single centre line is becoming more popular for a tempory mooring, or in locks. A line is taken from a centre ring around a bollard ashore and returned to the boat.

Visitor and permanent mooring sites usually have rings or bollards to moor to. Elsewhere you will need to use your mooring stakes and a hammer.

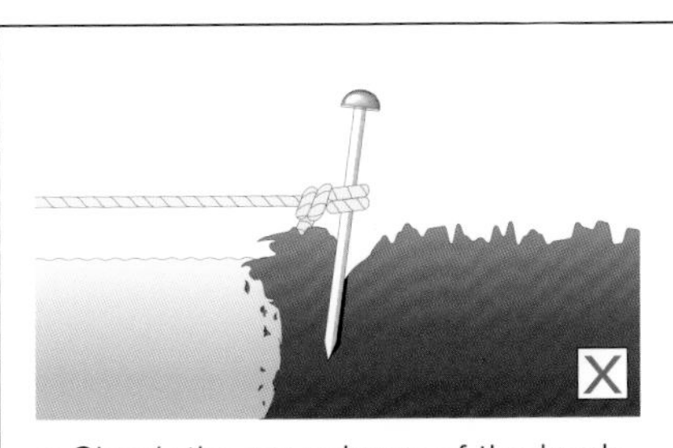

- Check the soundness of the bank, try to pick a stable section.
- Place the stakes away from the edge.

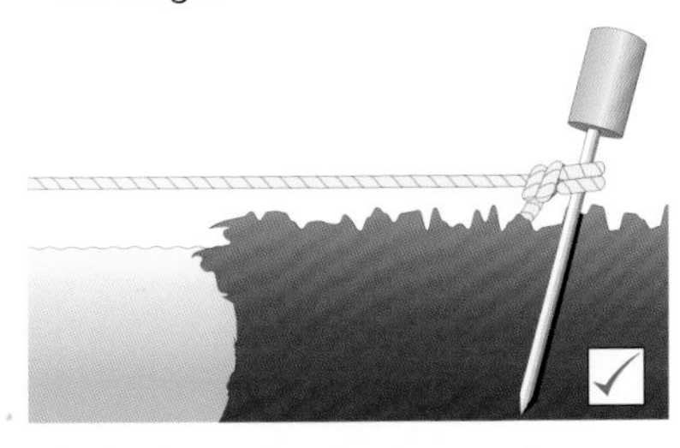

- Drive the stakes in at an angle away from the boat, to about three quarters of their length.
- Place an empty plastic bottle over the stake, to prevent passers-by tripping up.

- If your boat is not directly against the bank, use your gang plank – avoid jumping on or off the boat.

- Never stretch your mooring lines across the towpath, it could cause an accident.
- Avoid tying lines around trees, they can wear through the bark and kill the tree.
- At a popular mooring, move up close to the next boat rather than leave a gap.
- Be prepared to move up to accommodate other arrivals.
- If necessary, double up at popular places - always ask first.

- Don't pass the rope over the pulpit or stern rail. Take it from the cleat, through the fairlead (if you have one) and to the stake.
- Tie a clove hitch around the stake, then pass the rope back aboard, tying off on the cleat or dolly.
- Coil any spare rope up and stow it neatly
- Remember to put the hammer back on board.

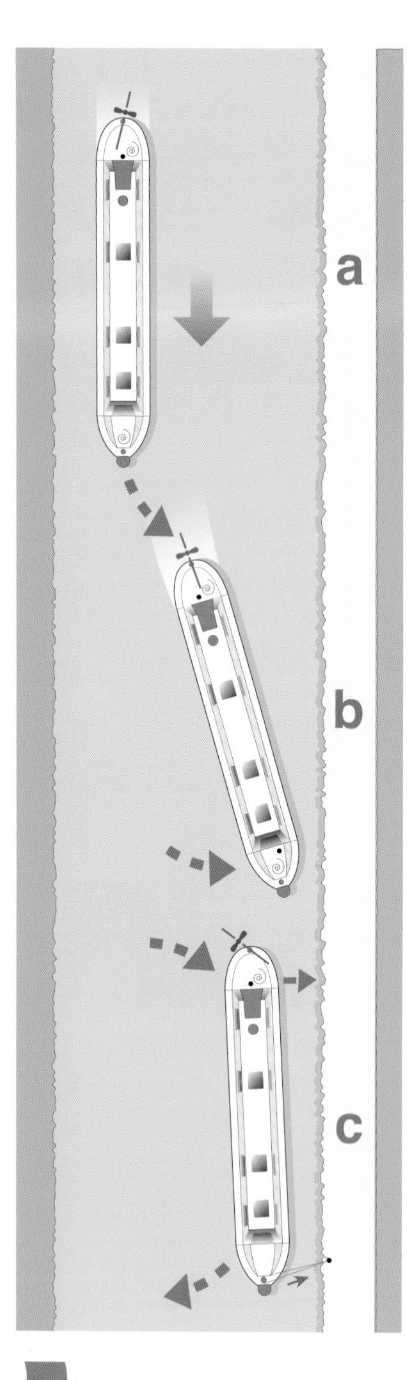

(**a**) Slow down well ahead of your intended mooring spot. Brief the crew.

Prepare the bow and stern lines and attach to their mooring cleats.

(**b**) Turn into the bank and use reverse gently to stop as the bow reaches the bank. Put engine in neutral.

The crew steps ashore with the bow line. Allow plenty of slack – do not pull the rope.

(**c**) Swing the stern in with the tiller hard over and using a short burst of forward revs.

Put the engine in neutral.

The shore crew ties off the bow line.

Pass the stern line to the shore crew (or step off with it yourself) and tie off.

Using a Centre Line

- Use the same procedure as in (**a**) but use a centre line instead.
- Have the centre line run forward to the front of the cabin roof.
- As the bow reaches the bank the crew steps ashore with the line.
- Pull on the line. (If possible, put around a bollard first). This pulls the boat into the bank.
- If more than a short stay, rig bow and stern lines as before.

(a) Start the engine in neutral.

Be aware of the wind direction.
Check for approaching craft.

Untie the stern line and withdraw the mooring stake. (If stuck, tap sideways with the mallet to make removal easier).

Coil the rope and put it on board with the stake.

(b) Untie the bow line and coil it.

Place the stake on board. Don't forget to put the mallet back onboard.

While the crew continues to hold the bow line, push the stern out into deep water.

(c) The crew steps onboard with the bow line and pushes the bow off with the boat pole.

When the bow is far enough out, motor ahead and get up to cruising speed (as quickly as possible if there is a side wind blowing).

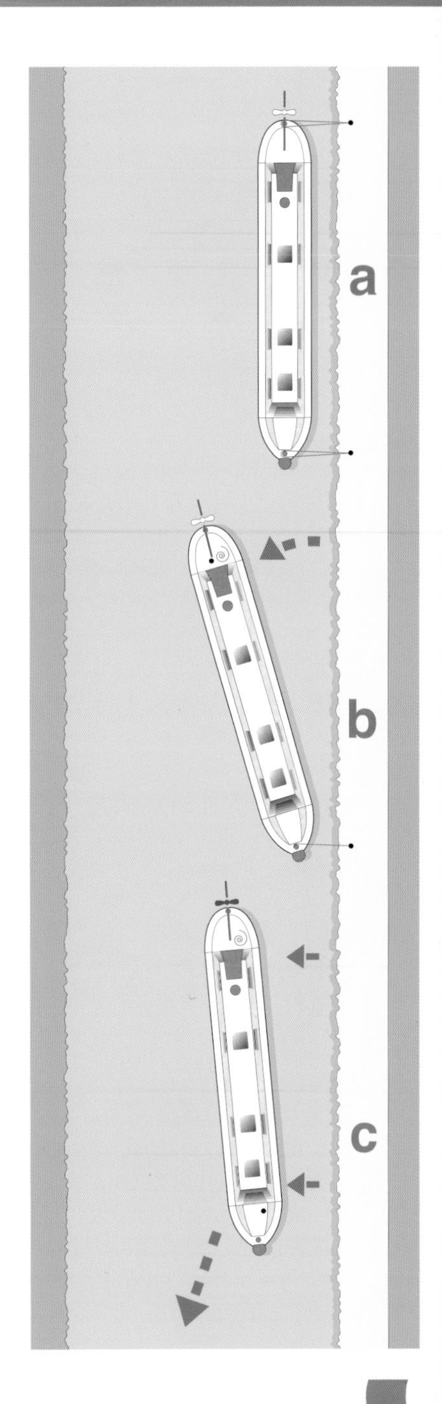

Don't just drive away from the bank or you may damage the prop.

Always push out into deeper water, using the pole if necessary.

REMEMBER: IT IS ALWAYS EASIER TO MOOR HEADING INTO THE CURRENT (OR WIND IF IT IS STRONGER).

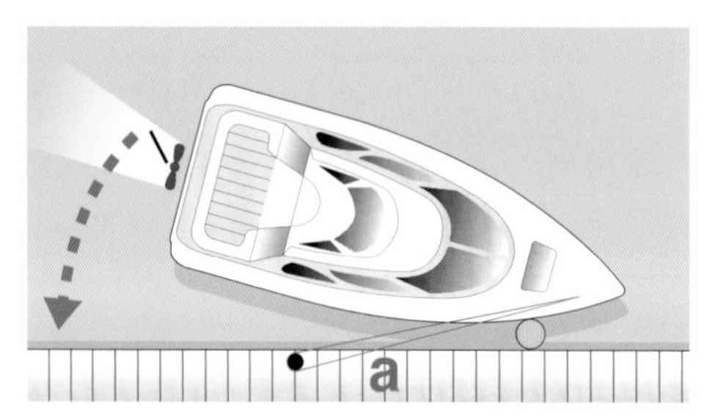

Single prop

- If space is tight or there's a strong offshore wind, use a spring line (**a**).
- Approach at a wide angle to the shore and secure the spring to a bollard.
- With a big fender at the bow, turn the rudder away from the shore and motor slowly ahead.
- The boat can't go forward, so she'll swing into the bank.

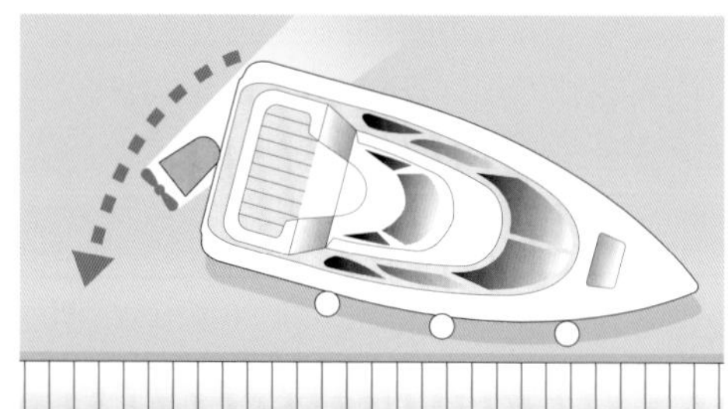

Single sterndrive

- Same procedure as single prop, if the gap is tight. If you have more room, just motor in at a gentle angle and put the engine into neutral.
- Then turn the helm towards the bank and apply astern power to pull the stern in.

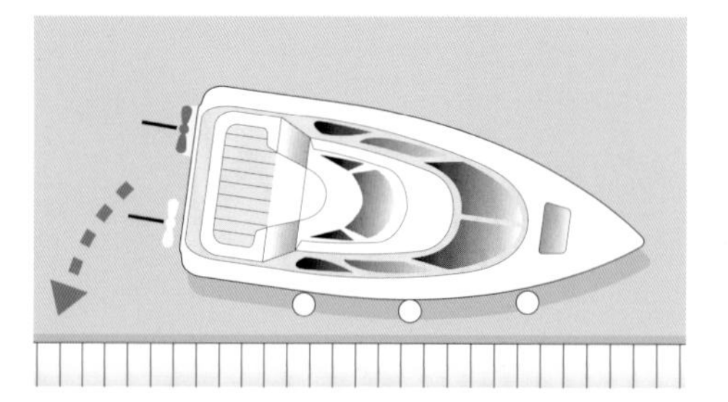

Twin props

Again, a spring can be used in a tight space but with practise the engines alone will get you in. If tick-over on both engines is too fast, use just the outside engine.

As you glide up to your chosen spot in neutral, put the outside engine in astern. This will swing the stern in.

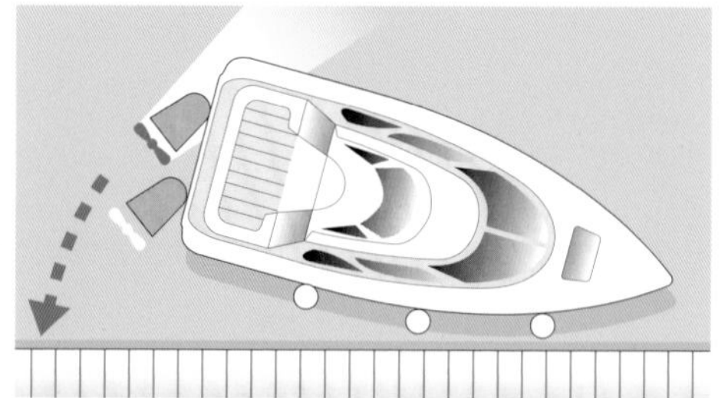

Twin Sterndrives

Use the same approach as twin props. Put the engines into neutral and see how she glides in. When alongside, turn the wheel towards the bank and engage astern on the outside engine.

REMEMBER: IT IS ALWAYS EASIER TO MOOR HEADING INTO THE CURRENT (OR WIND IF IT IS STRONGER).

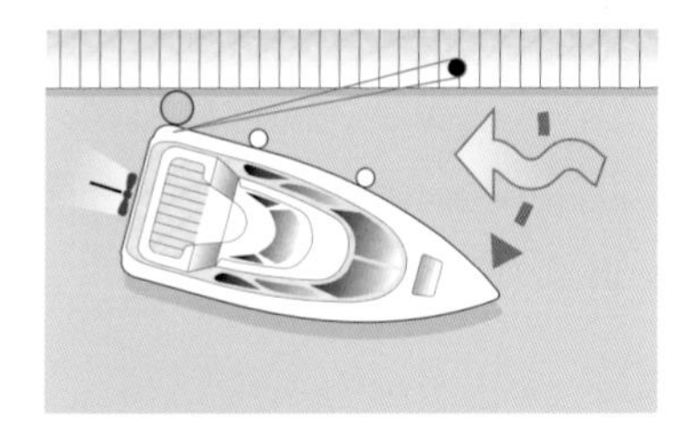

Single prop

If there's a strong current but not much room – rig a line from the stern, around a bollard and back to the boat. Release the bow and let the water flow push it out. Slip the line and motor away.

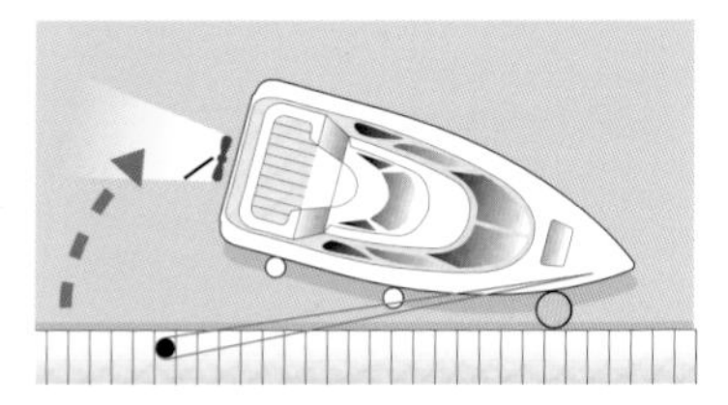

If there's a strong onshore wind and no current, rig the line at the bow and motor against it to swing the stern out.

Always use large fenders to protect the boat.

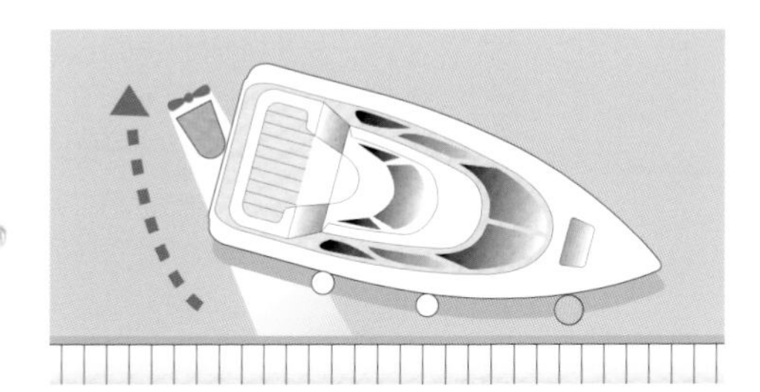

Single sterndrive

Use a spring in a tight space. Otherwise, turn the prop away from the bank, engage reverse and let it lift you off the bank as you back out.

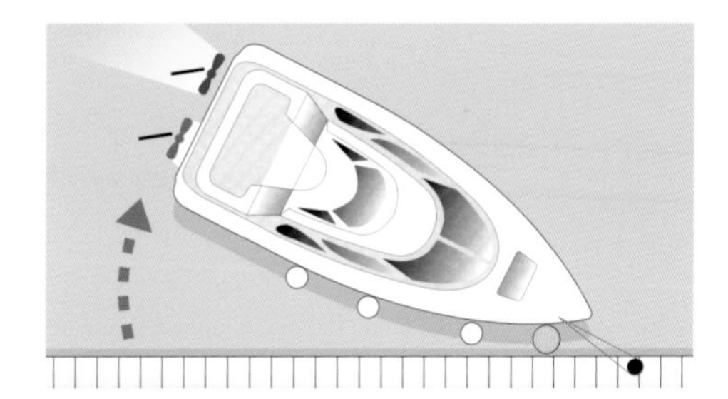

Twin props

Protect the bow with fenders and go astern on the inside prop. If there's an onshore wind you might need a touch of ahead from the outside prop or a bow line to pull against.

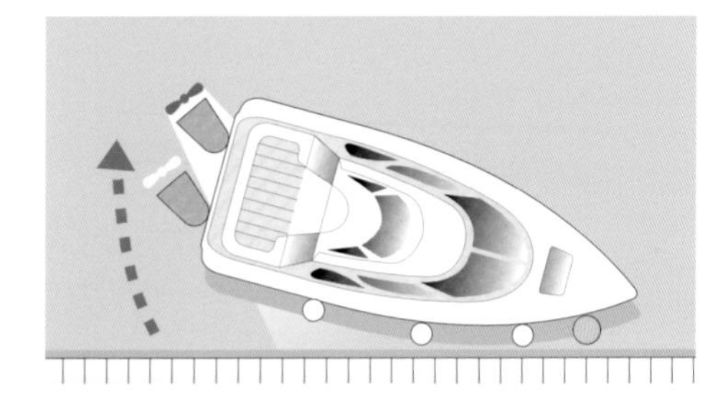

Twin sterndrive

Here is a case for not using opposite helm and engine. Turn the helm to the left and put the left engine in astern. This tends to lift the boat from the dock.

If shalllow, to avoid prop damage, use only the outside engine to gently drive her clear.

PARTS OF THE LOCK

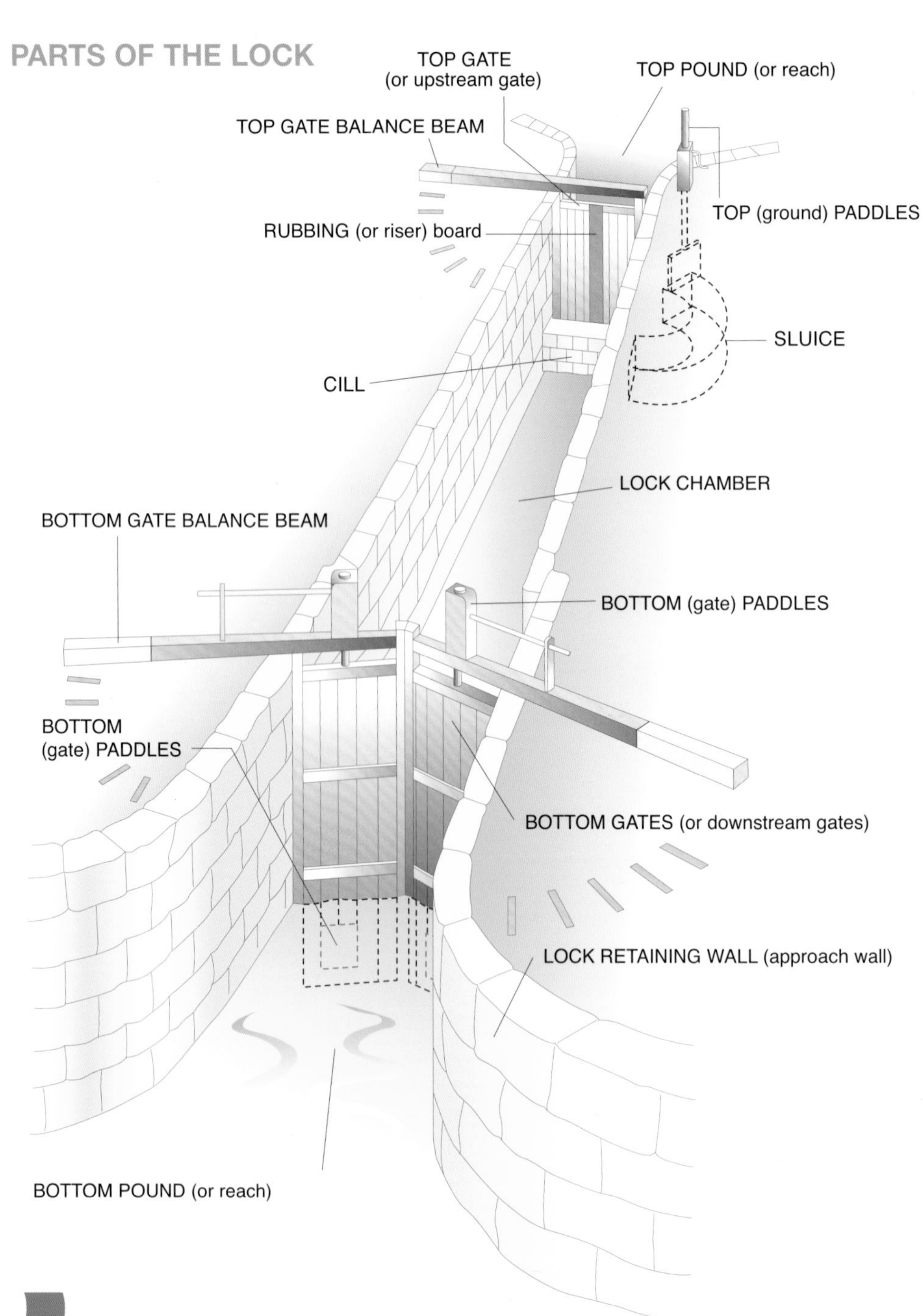

A lock is simply a chamber with gates at either end. By raising or lowering the water level in the chamber, you can go up or down hill. There are many types of lock but they all basically work in the same way:

- Empty the lock so the level is the same as your vessel.
- Open the gates.
- Enter the lock.
- Close the gates behind you.

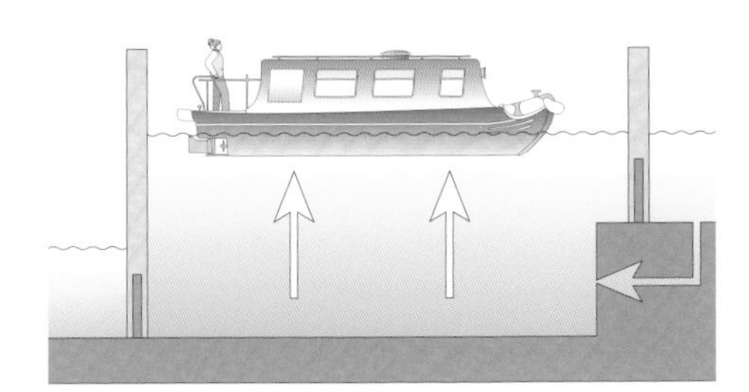

- Fill the lock by opening the appropriate sluices.
- When the water level is the same as the one you are moving to, open the gates.
- Exit the lock. Your boat has gone up a level.

Safety at locks

Working the locks is part of the fun of a waterways holiday but it is important to follow a few safety tips:

- When approaching a lock, never jump off the boat. Surfaces can be slippery and a fall between the boat and lock wall could be extremely dangerous.
- Always have a competent person on board.
- Never leave the boat unattended.
- Take your time – don't rush. Keep an eye open for problems.
- Make sure no one has their hands or feet dangling over the boat's side.
- Children should wear lifejackets, be fully supervised and kept well away from the edge.
- Ensure nobody is standing on the wrong side of the balance beam when the gates are being opened. Push gates open, its easier than pulling.
- When the water rushes in, it can be very noisy. Use hand communication signals which everyone knows beforehand.
- Keep the boat well away from the gates and cills.
- Make sure that the fenders do not get caught on anything.

IF SOMEONE FALLS INTO A LOCK YOU NEED TO ACT QUICKLY:

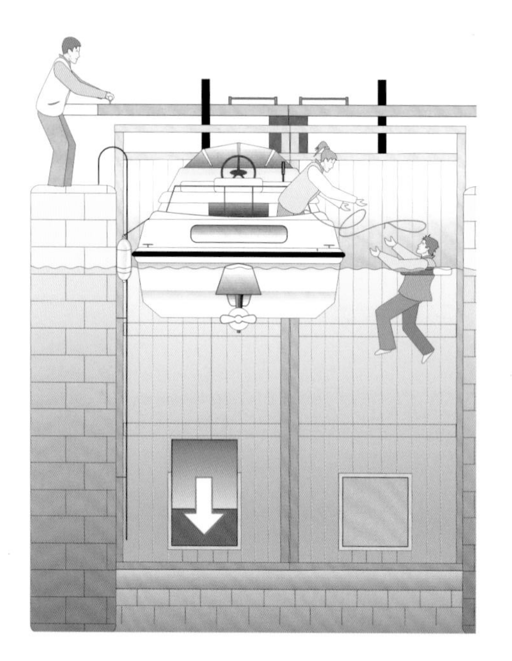

- Stop the engine.
- Close all the paddles.
- Throw a line or lifebelt to the MOB.
- Make sure that the boat cannot swing across and crush the MOB.
- Now consider the best way to get them out.
- Try to get the MOB to the ladder in the wall (all locks have them).
- All vessels should have a boarding ladder.
- If the MOB cannot climb out, you may need to slowly fill the lock to bring him up to your level.
- On many rivers there are lock keepers who are trained in rescue techniques. Always follow their instructions and assist as required.

Safe operation of paddle gear

- Make sure that the safety catch is in place before winding the handle.
- Check that the windlass is on the spindle properly. There is:
  - a parallel spindle on hydraulic paddles.
  - a tapered spindle on mechanical types.
- Wind the paddles up slowly but firmly. Never open more than a third initially, then assess water flow before opening further.
- Remove the windlass from the spindle after winding otherwise it may spin off at dangerously high speed. (No safety catches are necessary on hydraulic paddles).
- Keep fingers and clothing away from the paddle gearing.
- Always wind the paddle back down. If you let it drop it may shatter.

Paddle Gear

To operate locks, you will need a lock key (windlass) to wind up the paddles which open the sluice gates.
Paddle gear will be either mechanical (rack and pinion) or hydraulic.

On many large rivers, the lock keeper will control the locks.

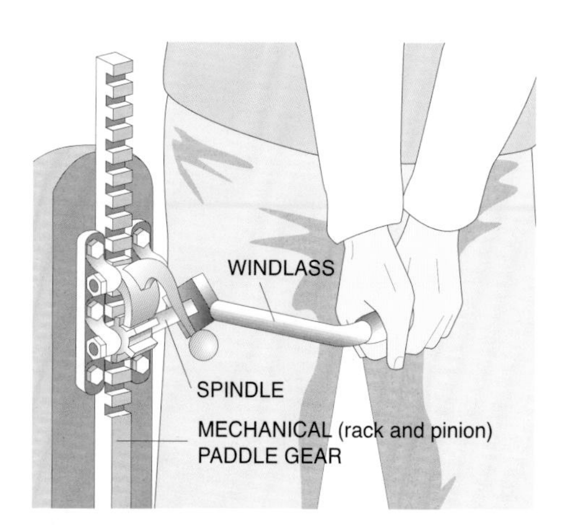

There are two main types of paddle:

Gate paddle (a)

A shutter over an underwater hole in the gate which, when raised, allows water to flow through. If the lock only has gate paddles, open maximum of a third initially, then assess water flow before opening further.

Ground paddle (b)

A shutter in a pipe (culvert) in the ground which, when raised, allows water to flow through.

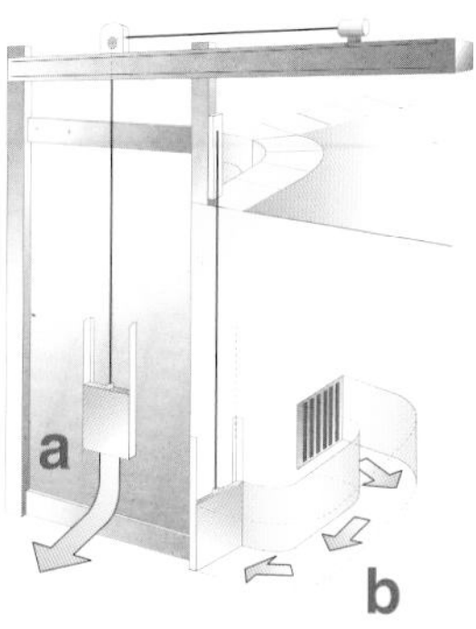

If a lock has both gate and ground paddles, always open the *ground paddle* **(1)** first. Do not open the gate paddle **(2)** until the shutter is underwater.

If you open the *gate paddle* first, you could flood your boat!

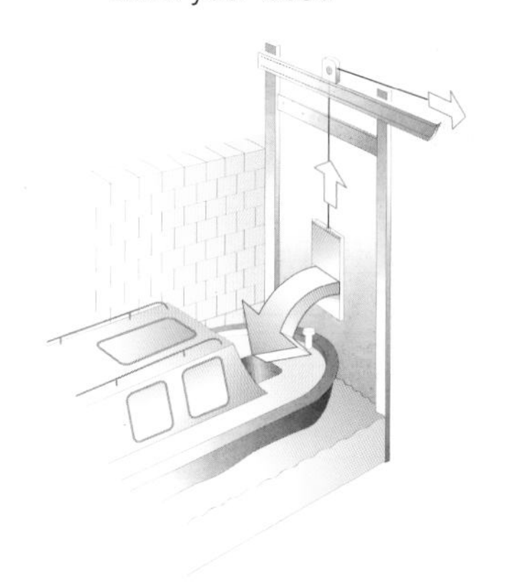

WORKING LOCKS REQUIRES TEAM WORK

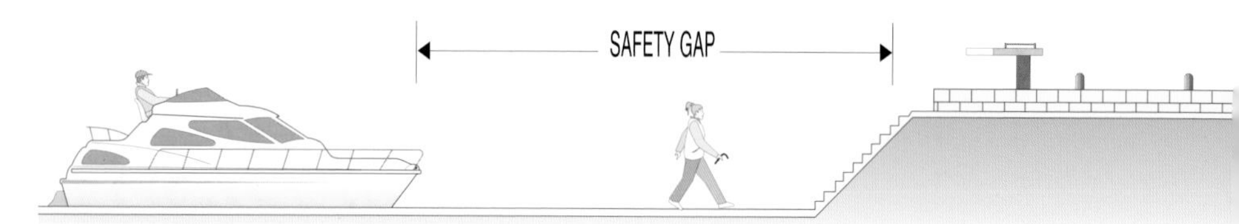

Going uphill

- As you approach a lock, drop a crew member off to go ahead and get the lock ready. If a boat is approaching downhill, they have priority.
- If the lock is empty, open the bottom gates and steer the boat straight in.
- If the lock is full, moor up far enough away to avoid the turbulence whilist the lock empties.
- If possible, hold a line around a bollard not just in your hand.
- Make sure that the top gates and paddles are closed.
- Open the bottom paddles.
- Now follow for narrow or broad locks.

Narrow locks

Narrow locks can accommodate one narrow beam boat, usually up to 70ft long.

Once in the lock, close the bottom gates and paddles. If there are bollards on the lockside, pass mooring lines up and round them. Don't tie them off.

Keep your engine going, using forward or reverse gear to control your position. If there are no bollards and the top gate has a rubbing board (a steel or wooden plate) rest the bow against it and put the engine in low forward gear to keep it there. (The bow may be against the lock cill to begin with).

Open the ground paddles at the top gate a couple of turns, pause - check the inflow of water - then another couple of turns. Open both paddles together if possible.

If the paddles are opened quickly, the turbulence created by the inrush of water will push you back, then draw you forward violently. This effect is more noticeable in deep locks. Use the mooring lines to hold the boat steady.

When the lock is half full, keep turning the paddles slowly until they are fully open.

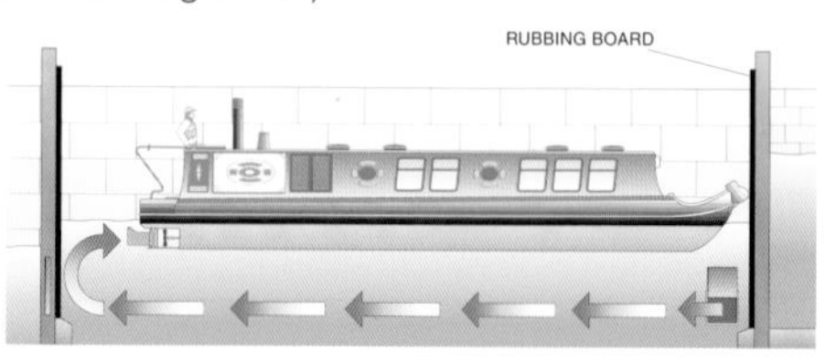

Make sure that your boat doesn't get caught on the gates. If it does, close the top paddles immediately. Now open a bottom paddle to lower the water level and free the boat.

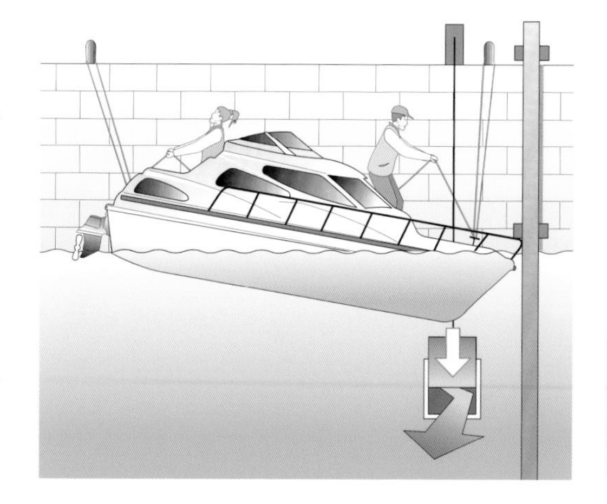

Do not tie or pass ropes around lock ladders or anything else inside the lock chamber. They will disappear underwater as the lock fills.

Broad locks.

Broad locks can usually hold two narrow boats side by side (breasted up) or one wider boat. Not all can take boats up to 70ft.

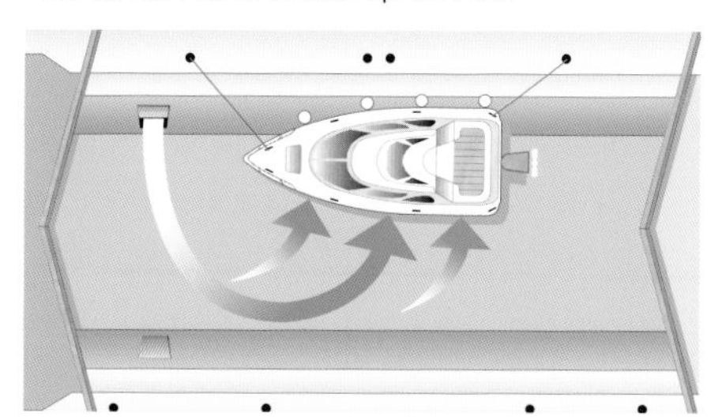

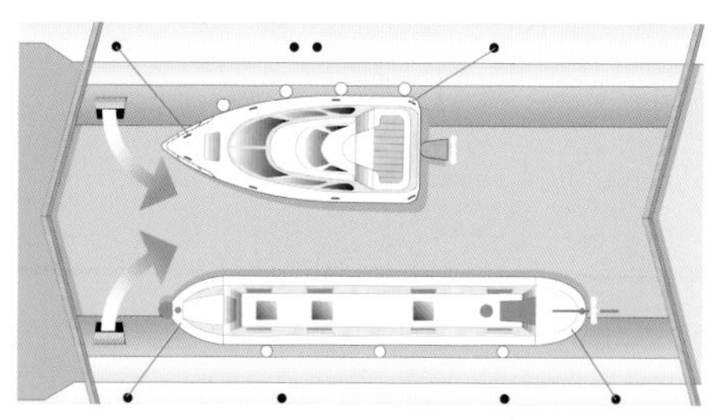

If you are the only boat working through a broad lock, open the ground paddle on the same side as the boat.

The flow of water will hold the boat alongside until the lock is about half full. Now you can open the other paddle.

Be careful that the bow doesn't swing out - hold it in with a line.

To conserve water, share a broad lock with another boat, if possible. If a narrowboat is sharing with a GRP boat, the narrowboat enters the lock first and the GRP boat exits first.

Ensure that the bows of both boats are level and open both paddles equally and progressively.

Use lines to hold the boats against the locksides- a centre line works well in canel locks.

Going downhill

- When approaching the lock, drop a crew member off to go ahead and prepare the lock.
- If the lock is empty, check for approaching craft coming uphill and let them use the lock first – it conserves water and is good manners.
- When the lock is free, make sure that the bottom paddles and gates are closed.
- Fill the lock by opening the top paddles.
- Close the top paddles and open the top gates.
- Enter the lock and close the top gates.
- Progressively open one, then the other, bottom paddle.

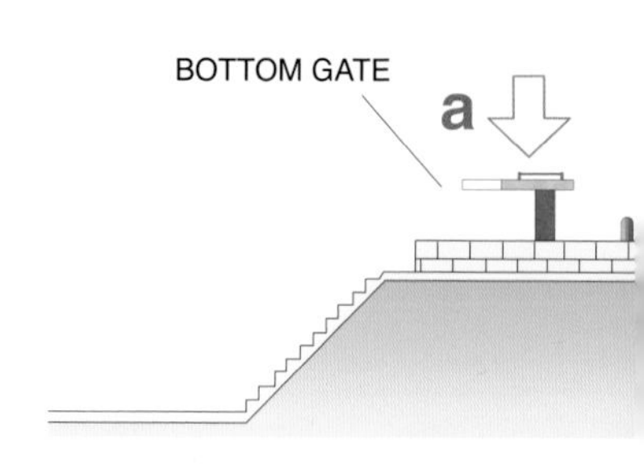

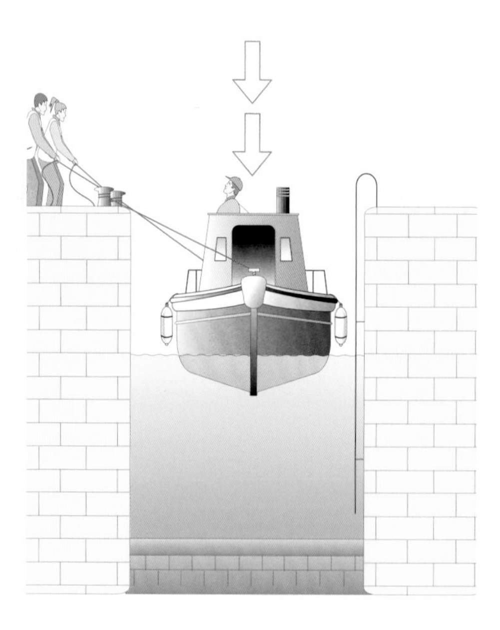

- As you descend, hold the boat steady with lines passed round bollards. Do not tie them off. Make sure they 'pay out' smoothly.
- Use your engine to keep the boat in position if necessary.
- Make sure that the boat's gunwales and guards do not catch on the lock edges as the boat goes down.
- When the lock is empty, open the bottom gates and exit.
- Close the bottom paddles.
- Close the gates (unless another boat is approaching).

On The Thames, engines must be turned off when stationery in locks.

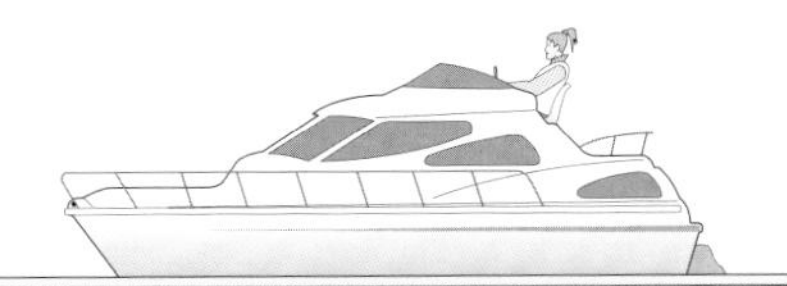

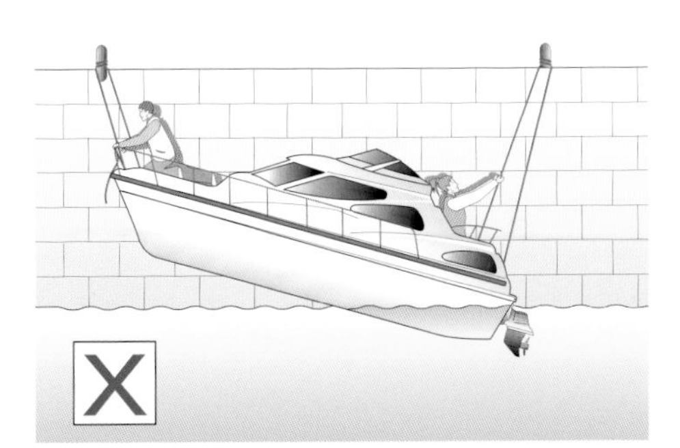

This is what can happen if you tie up in a lock

Do not cut the lines. Close the bottom paddles and refill lock to refloat the boat.

To avoid the sill, keep your boat's stern and rudder at least 6 feet away from the top gate.

On longer narrowboats (60ft plus) keep the bow as close to the bottom gate as possible (within 12") without actually touching the gate.

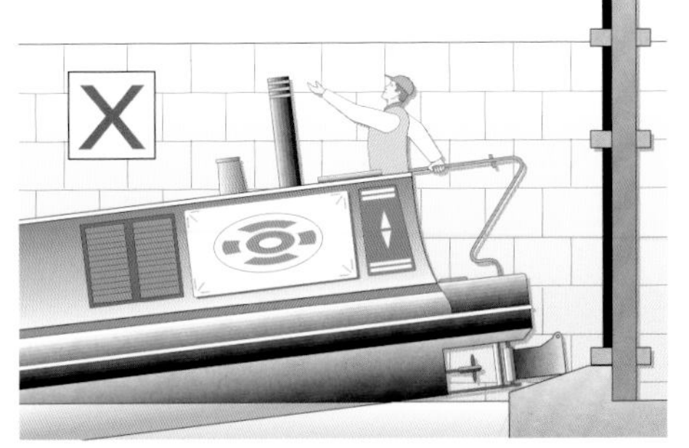

If your boat does get caught on the cill, close the bottom paddles immediately.

Open one top paddle gently. The boat will then float off.

Do not turn the prop until you are absolutely sure that there is no damage to the rudder, skeg or prop.

Conserving water

Each time a boat goes through a lock, up to 50,000 gallons of water are used. Canal reservoirs depend on rain to replenish supplies but in the summer, levels can get very low.

So follow the **THRIFT** Code:

Two in a lock. Share a lock whenever you can with another boat.
Have you shut all paddles and gates behind you?
Report any leaks or damage to the local navigation staff.
Invite any oncoming boats through if the lock is set against you.
Follow advice and instructions given by navigation staff.
Timings can change. Check for any lock restrictions and closures.

STAIRCASE LOCKS (FLIGHTS OF LOCKS)

Two, three, four, or even five locks joined together are called a staircase. The top gates of one lock are also the bottom gates of the next one.

There are two main types of staircase:

1. The water from the lock above flows into a side pond which then fills the lock below.
2. As illustrated, the water from each lock goes directly into the lock below. Most staircases are controlled by lock keepers. Always follow their directions. The rule is, only open one lock at a time.

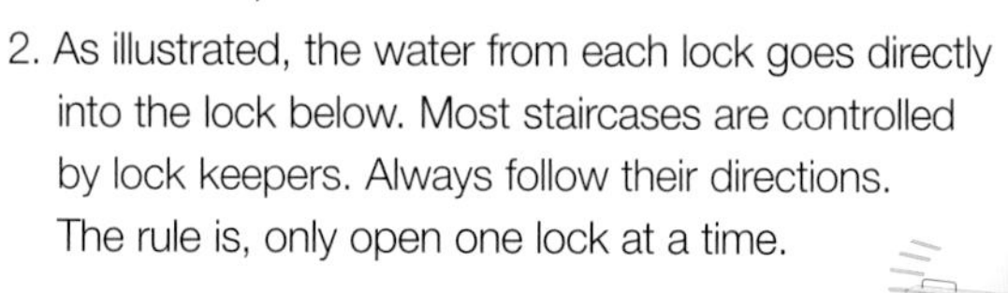

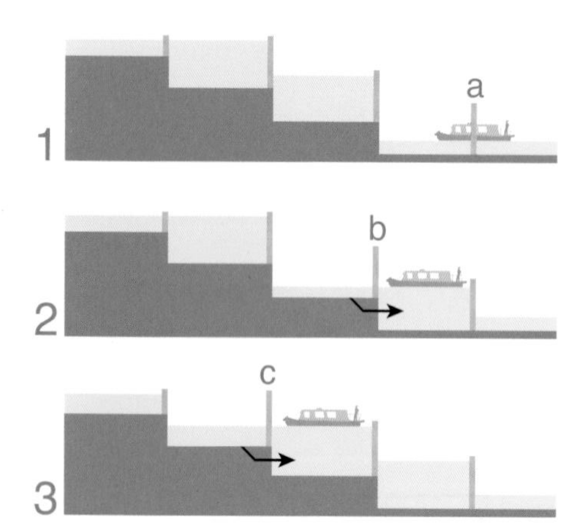

Going uphill

Prepare all the locks in a staircase before you enter the first lock. The bottom one should be empty, the rest full.

1. Enter the bottom lock and close the bottom gates and paddles (**a**).
2. Open the paddles (**b**) to fill the bottom lock from the middle lock.
   When the bottom lock is full, move into the middle lock. Close the gates and paddles behind you.
3. Open the paddles (**c**) of the next lock and repeat the process as before.

Going downhill

Prepare all the locks in the staircase before you enter the first lock. The top one should be full, the rest empty.

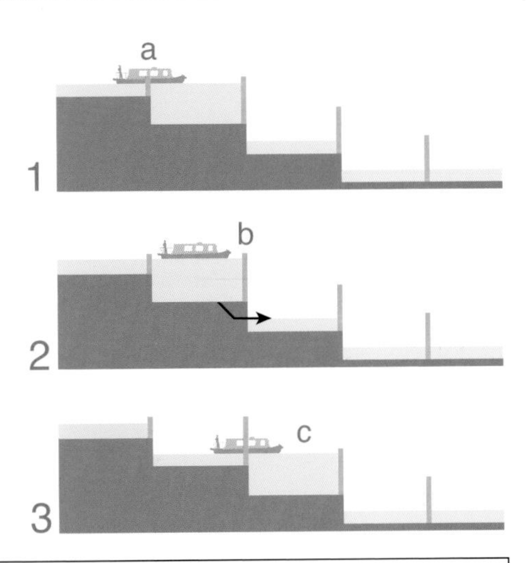

1. Enter the top lock and close the top gates and paddles behind you (**a**).
2. Open the bottom paddles (**b**). The water from the top lock will fill the middle lock.
3. When the top and middle lock levels are equal, move into the middle lock (**c**). Close the gates and paddles behind you and repeat the process as before.

PROBLEMS

Going downhill

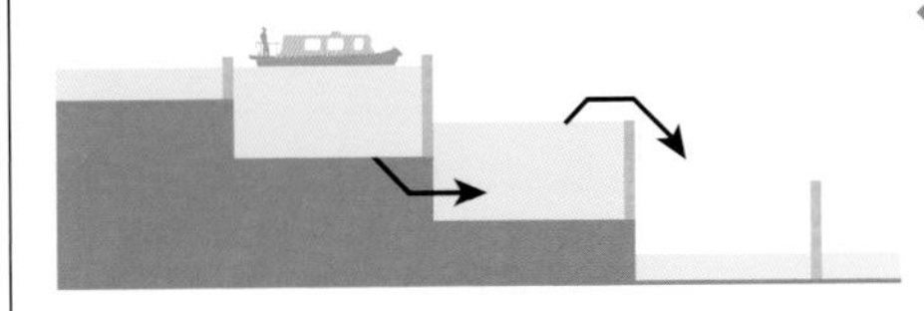

Make sure that the lower lock is empty enough to take all the water from above. If not, it will overflow.

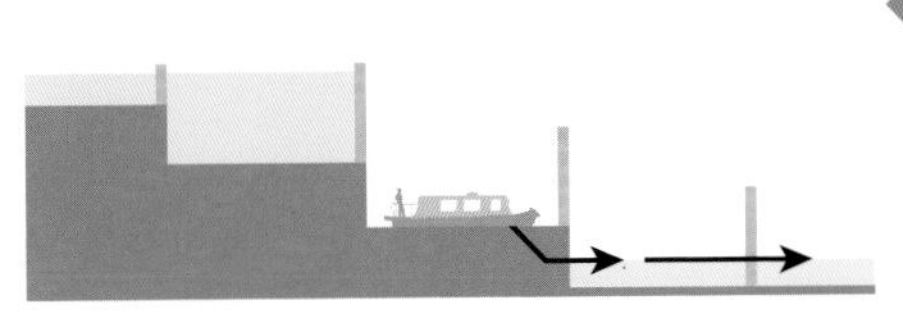

Always check that every gate and paddle behind you is closed before opening the paddles in front of you. If not, the lock above may completely drain. Also make sure that the paddles beyond the ones you are working on are closed otherwise the water will continue out through the next lock.

Going uphill

Make sure that the upper lock is full enough to fill the lock below. If not, you will run out of water. Check that every gate and paddle behind you is closed before opening the paddles in front of you. Otherwise you will lose all your water. After you have finished setting all the locks at the beginning, make sure that all paddles are closed.

Throughout your journey through the staircase, always check that every paddle and gate behind you is shut before opening those in front of you.
Don't worry if all this sounds complicated. Staircase locks are few and far between and almost all are keeper-operated during the summer months.

Guillotine locks

You will find lots of these locks on the River Nene and Great Ouse systems.

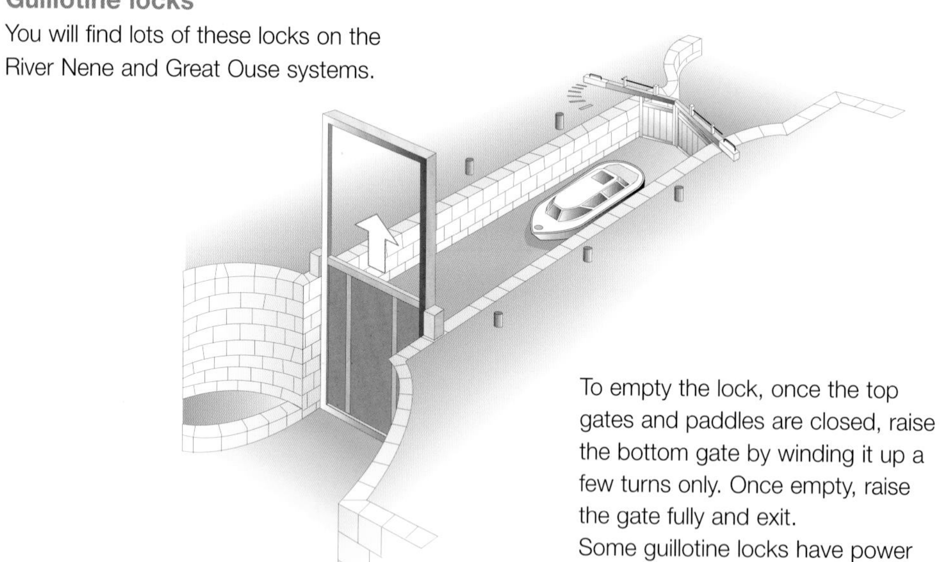

To empty the lock, once the top gates and paddles are closed, raise the bottom gate by winding it up a few turns only. Once empty, raise the gate fully and exit.
Some guillotine locks have power operation.

Twin locks

These can be either narrow or broad. You can use either lock but where possible use the one set in your favour.

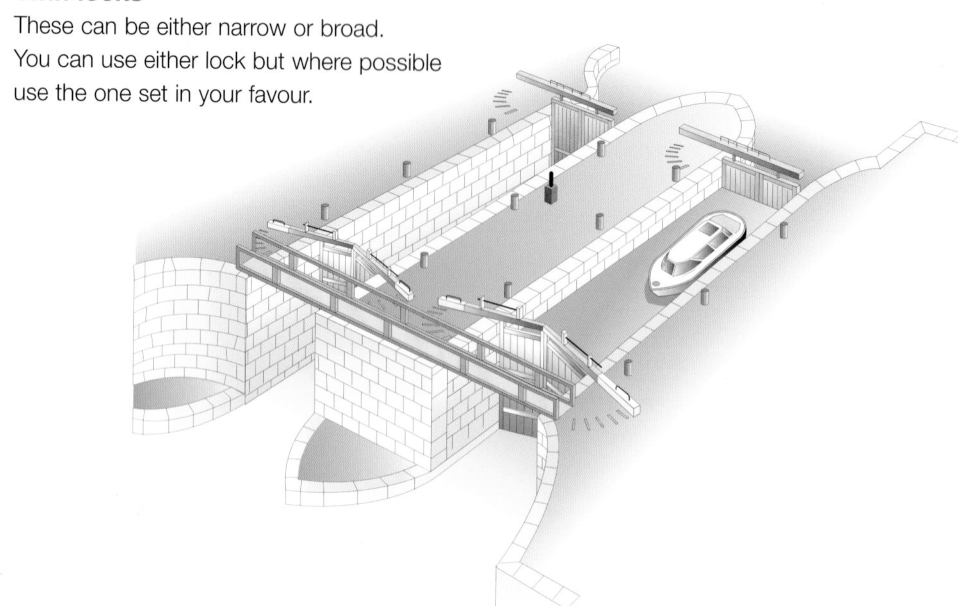

Larger locks

On commercial navigations and principal rivers such as the Thames and Severn, the locks are much larger than conventional ones. They are mostly keeper-operated and may have traffic lights. *(see p67)*.

Most are mechanised and some have limited opening hours. (Check the relevant guide book)

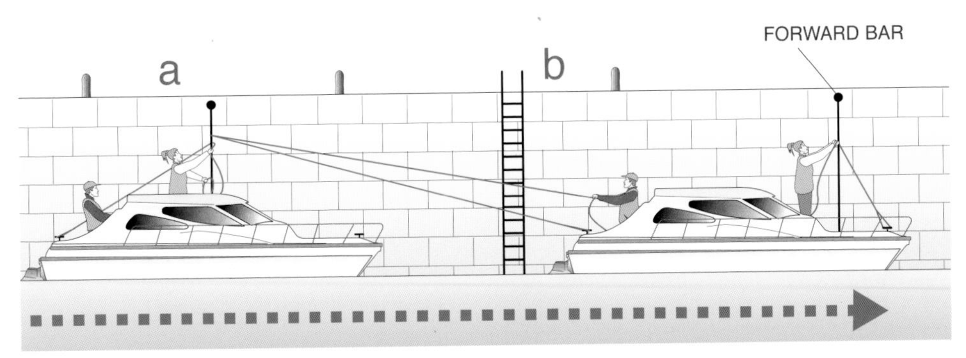

In the lock, bring the stern line forward (**a**) and pass around the bar or bollard in the lock wall, then motor forward, paying out the line (**b**). Pass the bow line round the forward bar or bollard, and centre your boat between the two points.

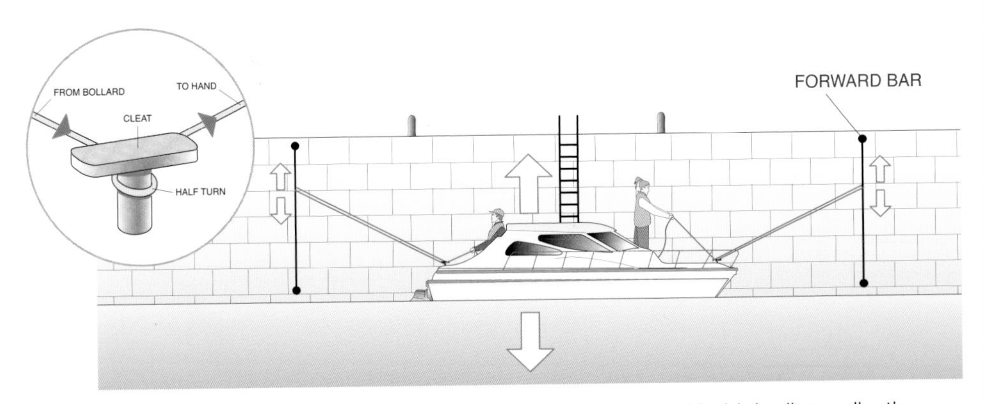

Do not tie the lines off. Take a half turn around your boat cleat and hold the line, adjusting as necessary.

Beware of the turbulence created as the paddles are raised. Keep the lines taut to prevent surging and adjust as necessary as you rise.

Going down is less turbulent. Pay out the lines as you descend making sure they do not jam.

WARN THE CREW TO BE AWARE OF LOW BRIDGES.

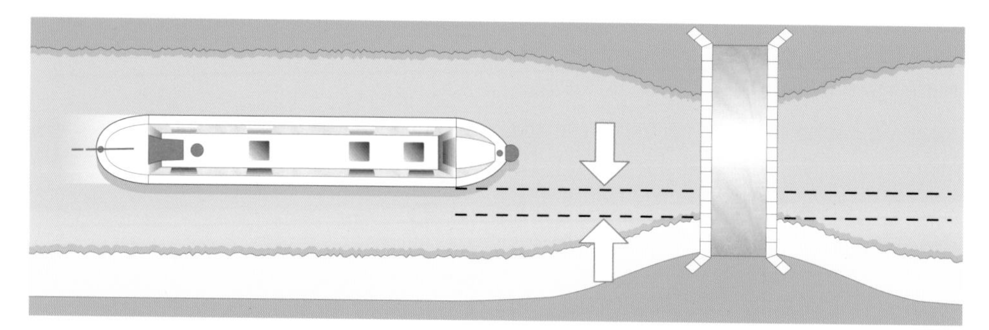

The channel narrows at bridges and the arch is usually lower on the non-towpath side.

Take down vulnerable chiminies, aerials, etc.

Check for any boats coming the other way. If the other boat is nearer, give way. Slow down early, keep to the right and wave them on.

Resume your course when they have passed. If you have to stop, don't reverse too hard, or your boat may turn sideways (broach) and block the channel.

Line the boat up early and look along the side of the boat. Aim to miss the towpath through the bridge by 6-12 inches.

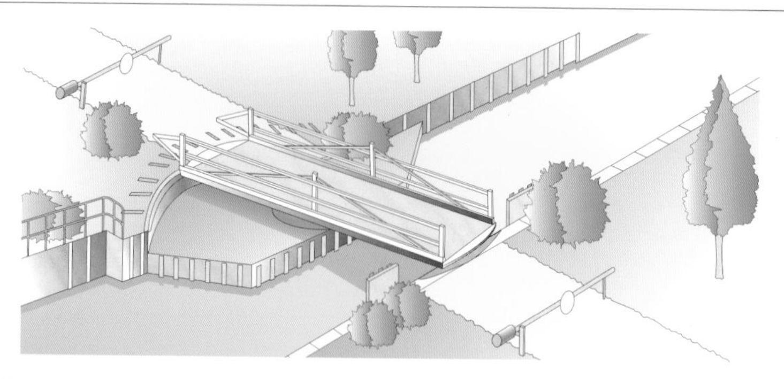

Swing bridge

Well before the bridge, land your crew (with windlass and/or key). If it is a heavy manual bridge, you may need more than one crew.

If it is a traffic bridge, check that the road is clear. Many have traffic barriers which must be closed before the bridge is opened.

Unhook the retaining chain or hasp and steadily push the bridge open.

Slow the bridge down as it reaches the end of the swing so that it doesn't bounce back across the canal.

Once the boat is through, shut the bridge and secure it with the chain or hasp.

Don't forget to re-open the traffic safety barriers before you get back on board.

Lifting bridge

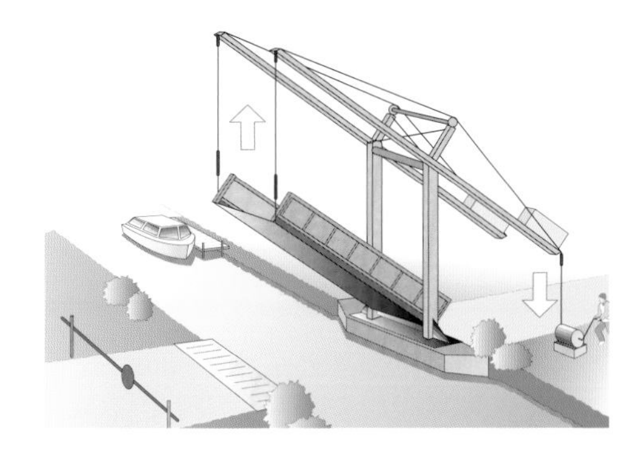

- Well before the bridge, land your crew (with windlass and/or key).
- If it is a traffic bridge, check that the road is clear and close the barriers.
- Pull the chain down and sit on the beam to hold the bridge open. This is very important - bridges have been known to fall on boats.
- On winch drum or hydraulic bridges, make sure that any latches or catches are in place.
- When the boat is through, gently lower the bridge. Do not let it drop.
- Re-open the traffic barriers and re-board the boat.

Mechanised bridge

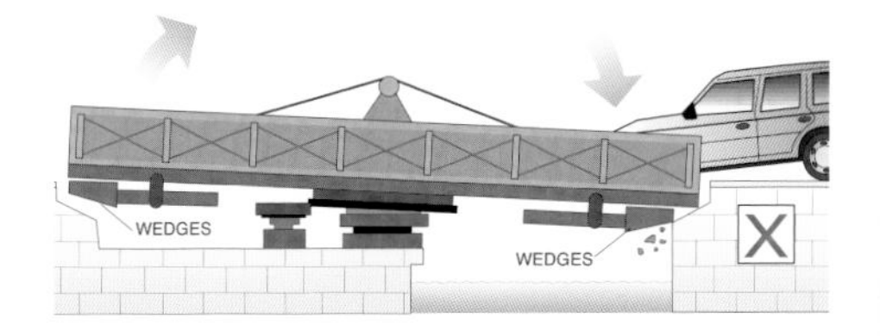

These bridges vary greatly; some are windlass-operated, others are powered and need a BW Watermate key.

On larger waterways, they are controlled by keepers and have traffic lights *(see p67)*. For self-operated bridges, follow the instructions.

Most modern bridges have wedges so they don't bounce when vehicles cross. Follow the instructions to release these before operating the bridge.

Make sure the wedges are back in their original place before leaving otherwise vehicles may damage the mechanism.

Movable bridge safety tips

- Drop crew off sufficiently early enough for you to manoeuvre into the centre of the channel before passing through the bridge.
- Make sure that there is nobody on the roof, foredeck or in the well deck as you pass through.
- Watch out for crosswinds.
- Don't let the boat arrive too early – if the bridge is not properly open there will be no time to stop before a dangerous collision.

Never allow children or passers-by to operate the bridge for you.

Safety tips

Put your tunnel light and cabin lights on with curtains open to illuminate the tunnel.

Keep heads, arms and legs well Inside the boats profile.

Watch out for reduced headroom in the middle.

Height gauges are placed at both entrances of low tunnels. If your boat's cabin hits the gauge, do not proceed – you may get wedged halfway through!

Tunnels vary in length and width: in some, two narrowboats can pass, in others, there is only room for one. Check at the entrance for any special instructions.

If there is another boat in the tunnel, wait unless you know you can pass. Obey any traffic lights. Extinguish all naked flames except pilot lights.

Stay in the centre in the tunnel.
Don't move the tiller too much.

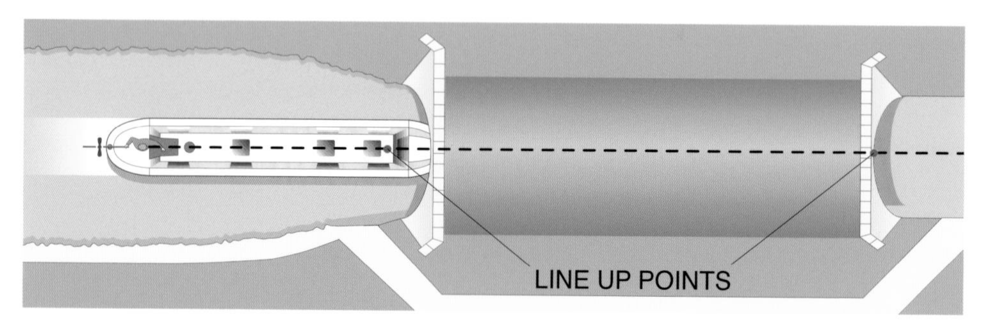

It's common to feel that you are going to one side. Keep a point on the cabin top in line with the pin point of light at the other end. Don't over-compensate or you will zig-zag badly.
In wide tunnels, look out for approaching craft. Slow right down and pass on the right.
Keep your light on until you've come out at the other end, to warn approaching boats.

Do not stop unless you break down. If you do have to stop:

- Turn the engine off to avoid fumes building up.
- Sound long horn blasts to attract attention.
- If you can't cure the problem, push the boat out. Use the boat poles or walk the boat along by pushing off the walls.
- Luminous arrows in the roof show the shortest way out.
- Do not swim out.

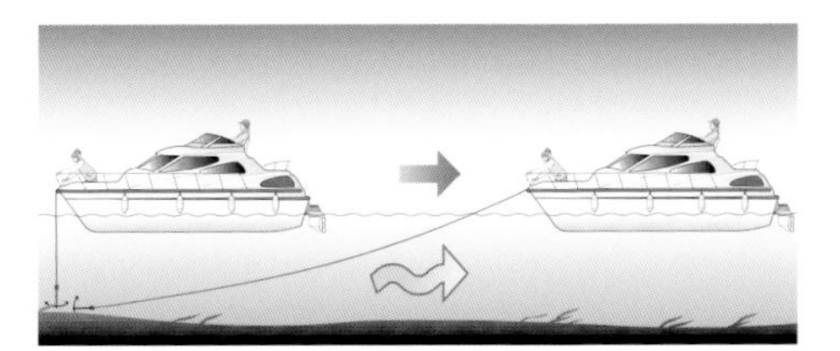

Dropping the anchor

Have the anchor rope ready (about 6 times the depth of water) to pay out as soon as the boat stops.

Drop the anchor and reverse back slowly paying out the line.

When the correct amount is out, make fast and apply a little extra power astern to help the anchor dig in.

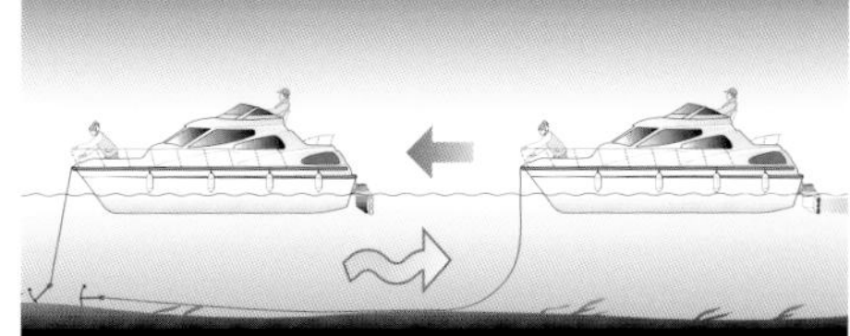

Getting the anchor up (weighing anchor)

Often, the crew can just pull the line in, but in a strong wind or current, a touch of ahead will take the load off as the crew pulls in the slack.

If the anchor is stuck, make the anchor line fast when the rope is upright and let the momentum of the boat break it out of the bottom.

On a narrow fast flowing waterway, keep the anchor at the upstream end of the boat to act as a brake in an emergency.

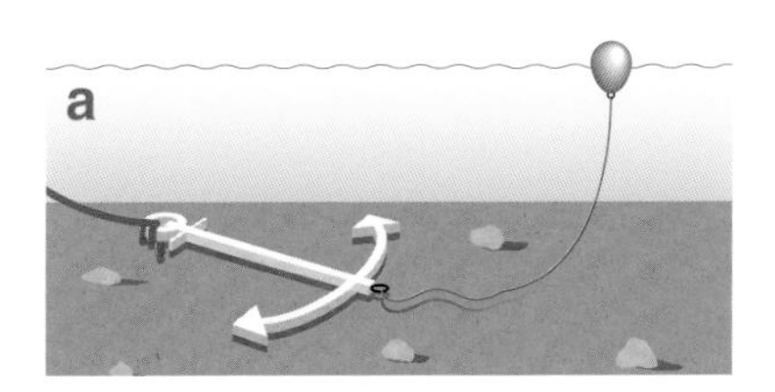

If you think the anchor may get stuck, add a tripping line (**a**) to the other end of the anchor so you can pull it free.

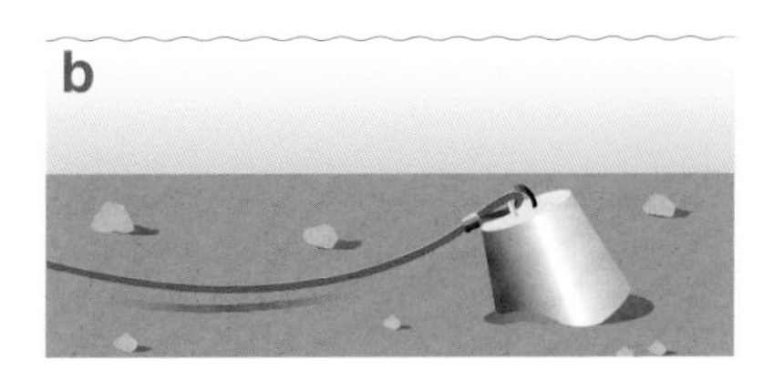

A mud weight (**b**) is often used as a non-snagging anchor when there's little or no current.

Hire boats are not allowed to navigate after dark.
Cruising in the dark can be dangerous and the inexperienced are advised not to.

On rivers, all boats must have navigation lights.

On canals, a narrow boat must have at least a white light showing to the front.

Note that a tunnel light is not the same as a navigation light.

Take extra care if using locks at night. Accidents are far more likely and it is easy to inadvertently leave a paddle up and waste water.

Navigation Lights

A WHITE light front and back

A **GREEN** light on the right (starboard) side

A **RED** light on the left (port) side

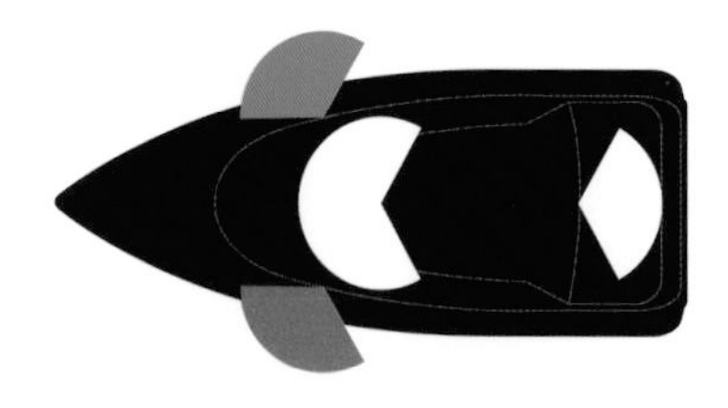

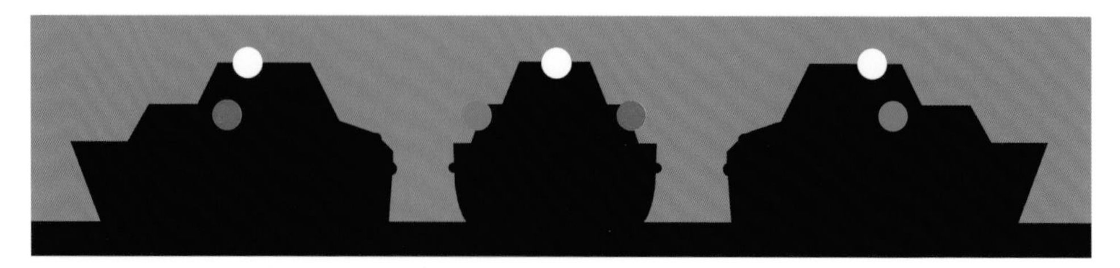

These navigation lights can tell you which way another boat is going:

White above red – crossing from right to left.
White above green and red – coming towards you.
White above green – crossing from left to right.

Note: small boats may show a single all round white light or a combined red/green bow light.

THESE ARE THE USUAL SOUND SIGNALS. CHECK YOUR LOCAL WATERWAYS BOOK FOR MORE INFORMATION. BE PREPARED, OTHERS MIGHT NOT KNOW THEIR MEANING.

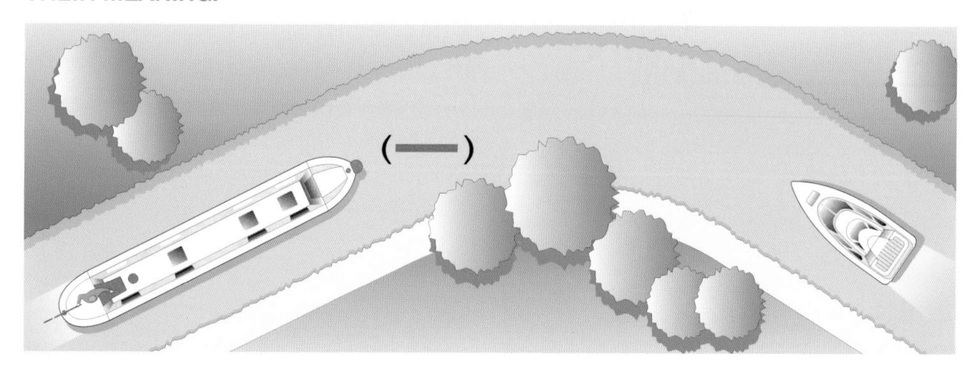

Sound a long blast every 20 seconds when approaching a blind bend or bridge. Position a crew member forward as a look-out.

MAKE SURE THAT OTHERS KNOW YOUR INTENTIONS:

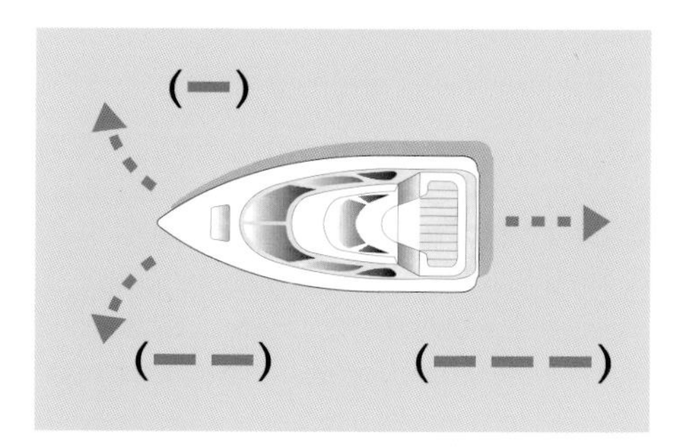

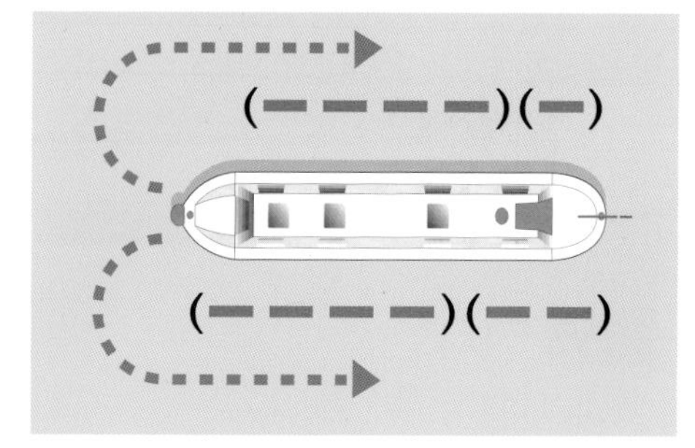

(—)

One short blast
I AM TURNING TO THE RIGHT (STARBOARD)

Two short blasts
I AM TURNING TO THE LEFT (PORT)

Three short blasts
I AM TRYING TO REVERSE (GOING ASTERN)

(——)

One extra long blast
WARNING AT TUNNELS, BLIND BENDS AND JUNCTIONS

(— — — —)(—)

Four short blasts, pause, then one short blast
I AM TURNING AROUND TO MY RIGHT (STARBOARD)

(— — — —)(— —)

Four short blasts, pause, then two short blasts
I AM TURNING AROUND TO MY LEFT (PORT)

(— — — — —)

Five or more short blasts
YOUR INTENTIONS ARE UNCLEAR OR ARE YOU TAKING SUFFICIENT AVOIDING ACTION.

On some British rivers and canals, lock keepers can be contacted by VHF radio. This is more common abroad.

If using VHF, at least one person on board must hold a Restricted Operator's Certificate. It is also a requirement for every boat fitted with a VHF radiotelephone to be covered by a Ship Radio Licence which is renewable annually.

Ship radio licences are issued by:

Radio Licensing Centre, PO Box 1495, Bristol, BS99 3QS

Tel: 0870 243 4433
Email: ams@ra.gsi.gov.uk

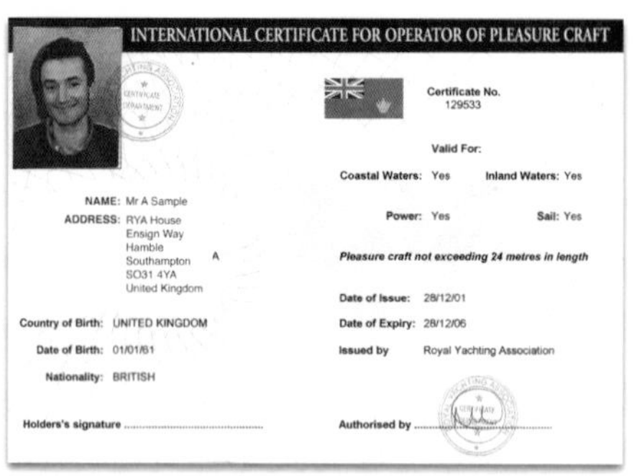

INTERNATIONAL CERTIFICATE FOR OPERATOR OF PLEASURE CRAFT

Certificate No. 129533

Valid For:

Coastal Waters: Yes Inland Waters: Yes

Power: Yes Sail: Yes

Pleasure craft not exceeding 24 metres in length

NAME: Mr A Sample
ADDRESS: RYA House
Ensign Way
Hamble
Southampton
SO31 4YA
United Kingdom

Country of Birth: UNITED KINGDOM
Date of Birth: 01/01/61
Nationality: BRITISH

Date of Issue: 28/12/01
Date of Expiry: 28/12/06
Issued by Royal Yachting Association

Holders's signature ....

Authorised by ....

EUROPEAN REQUIREMENTS

In other European countries, there are a number of requirements for vessels using inland waterways. For example you may be required to carry a copy of the Inland waterway rules (CEVNI).

All British vessels also have to be registered if cruising outside British waters and an International Certificate of Competence (ICC) may be necessary.

For more information on any of the above, contact the RYA on 0845 345 0400 or visit their website: www.rya.org.uk

When going upstream, **red** buoys or cylindrical markers define the port (left) side of the channel. Posts can be all red, or have white bands. A flashing red light may show at night.

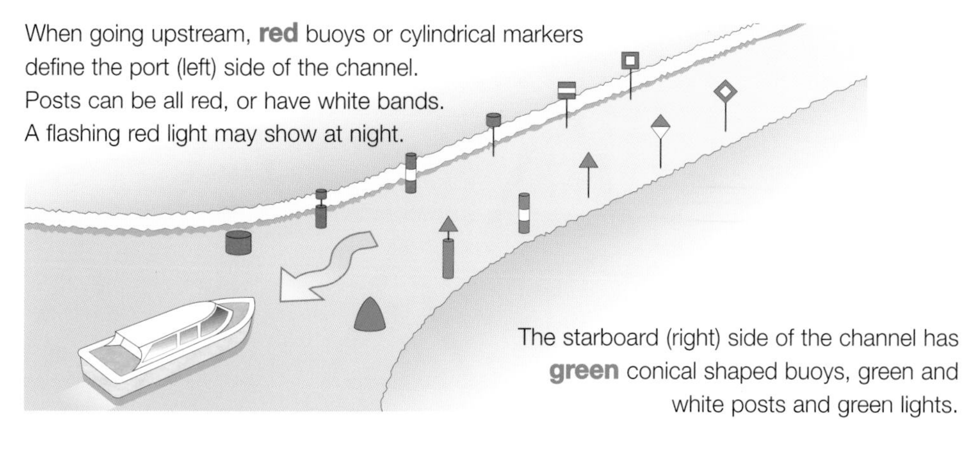

The starboard (right) side of the channel has **green** conical shaped buoys, green and white posts and green lights.

BUOYS AND LIGHTS ARE THE OTHER WAY ROUND WHEN GOING DOWNSTREAM

TRAFFIC LIGHTS

When used at locks and bridges Traffic lights have similar meanings to those used on highways and must be obeyed.

RED
STOP
do not pass this light

RED and **GREEN**
GET READY TO PROCEED
but do not pass the red light

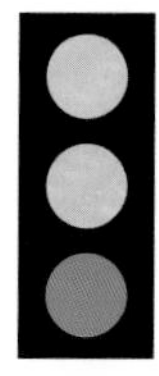

GREEN
GO

AMBER
PROCEED WITH CAUTION

DREDGING OR WORKS

Pass the dredger on the side showing the white or green lights or diamond shapes. Do not pass on the side showing red lights or ball shapes. But, beware: on canals, the edges of works or restrictions on both sides are often marked with red lights or red squares by day irrespective of whether you are going upstream or downstream.

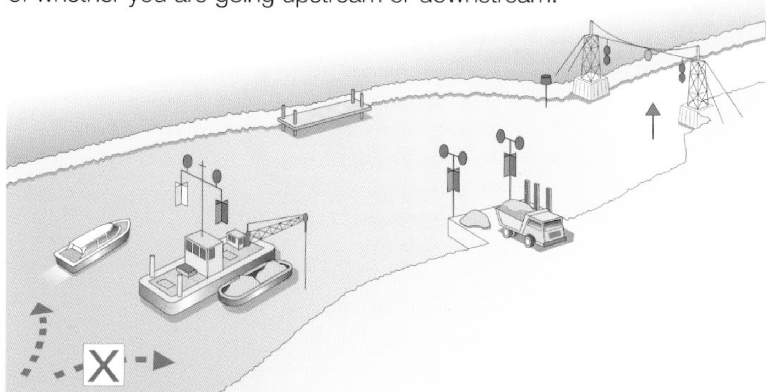

WARNING SIGNS

Weir

Ferry

Overhead cable

Headroom limited

Depth limited

Width limited

PROHIBITORY SIGNS

No entry

No

No overtaking

No anchoring

No mooring

No pump out

No refuse disposal

No turning

Do not create wash

No fishing

No motor boats

No swimming

No shooting

MANDATORY SIGNS

Beware

Use this radio channel

Sound horn

Speed limit

Move over or turn in this direction

One-way

Cross channel to left

Cross channel to right

Keep to the side of the channel on your left side

Keep to the side of the channel on your right side

INFORMATIVE SIGNS

Water (cold)

Refuse disposal

Chemical closet disposal unit

Mooring
often with time limit

Telephone

Toilets

Winding point

Tunnel

Disabled

Water tap

Toilet pump out

Showers

Turning place

Lifting bridge

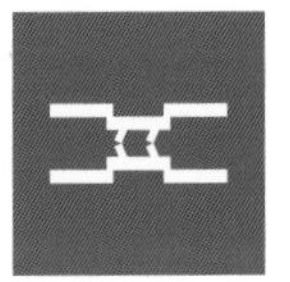
Lock

Different navigation authorities may use different regulations. Make sure you have a copy of the relevant reference books on board. In mainland Europe most countries use a common system based on CEVNI.

Promoting

The RYA is the national organisation which represents the interests of everyone who goes boating for pleasure.

The greater the membership, the louder our voice when it comes to protecting members' interests.

Apply for membership today, and support the RYA, to help the RYA support you.

and Protecting Boating

Benefits of Membership

- Access to expert advice on all aspects of boating from legal wrangles to training matters
- Special members' discounts on a range of products and services including boat insurance, books, videos and class certificates
- Free issue of certificates of competence, increasingly asked for by everyone from overseas governments to holiday companies, insurance underwriters to boat hirers
- Access to the wide range of RYA publications, including the quarterly magazine
- Third Party insurance for windsurfing members
- Free Internet access with RYA-Online
- Special discounts on AA membership
- Regular offers in RYA Magazine
- ...and much more

Join online at *www.rya.org.uk*
or use the form overleaf.

Visit the website for information, advice, member services and web shop.

If you have previously been a member and know your membership number please enter here

When completed, please send this form to: RYA RYA House Ensign Way Hamble Southampton SO31 4YA

	Tick box	Cash/Chq.	DD
Family†		£44	£41
Personal		£28	£25
Under 21		£11	£11

Please indicate your main area of interest

- ❑ *Yacht Racing*
- ❑ *Yacht Cruising*
- ❑ *Dinghy Racing*
- ❑ *Dinghy Cruising*
- ❑ *Personal Watercraft*
- ❑ *Inland Waterways*
- ❑ *Powerboat Racing*
- ❑ *Windsurfing*
- ❑ *Motor Boating*
- ❑ *Sportsboats and RIBs*

These prices are valid until 30.10.03 † Family Membership = 2 adults plus any U21s all living at the same address.

For details of Life Membership and paying over the phone by Credit/Debit card, please call 0845 345 0374/5 or join online at www.rya.org.uk

PLEASE USE BLOCK CAPITALS

	Title	Forename	Surname	Date of Birth	Male	Female
1.						
2.						
3.						
4.						

Address

Town County Postcode

Home Phone No. Day Phone No.

Facsimile No. Mobile No.

Email Address

Signature Date

RYA

Instructions to your Bank or Building Society to pay by Direct Debit

DIRECT Debit

Please fill in the form and send to:
RYA RYA House Ensign Way Hamble Southampton SO31 4YA Tel: 0845 345 0400

Name and full postal address of your Bank/Building Society

To The Manager Bank/Building Society

Address

Postcode

Name(s) of Account Holder(s)

Bank/Building Society account number

Branch Sort Code

Originator's Identification Number

9	5	5	2	1	3

Reference Number

Instruction to your Bank or Building Society
Please pay Royal Yachting Association Direct Debits from the account detailed in this instruction subject to the safeguards assured by The Direct Debit Guarantee. I understand that this instruction may remain with the Royal Yachting Association and, if so, details will be passed electronically to my Bank/Building Society.

Signature(s)

Date

Banks and Building Societies may not accept Direct Debit Instructions for some types of account

OR YOU CAN PAY BY CHEQUE

Source Code
077

Cheque enclosed £

Made payable to the Royal Yachting Association

Office use only: Membership number allocated